Get That
INTERVIEW!

Get That
INTERVIEW!

By R. Theodore Moock, Jr.

THE
INDISPENSABLE
GUIDE
FOR
COLLEGE
GRADS

BARRON'S

All inquiries should be addressed to:
Barron's Educational Series, Inc.
250 Wireless Boulevard
Hauppauge, New York 11788

Library of Congress Catalog Card No. 95-40585

International Standard Book No. 0-8120-9561-8

Library of Congress Cataloging-in-Publication Data
Moock, R. Theodore.
    Get that interview : the indispensable guide for college
grads / by R. Theodore Moock, Jr.
        p. cm.
    Includes index.
    ISBN 0-8120-9561-8
    1. Job hunting. 2. Résumés (Employment) 3. College
graduates—Employment. I. Title.
HF5382.7.M636   1996
650.14—dc20   95-40585
                                                  CIP

PRINTED IN THE UNITED STATES OF AMERICA
6789 8800 987654321

Table of Contents

PART TWO: PREPARING FOR THE INTERVIEW SEARCH

PART THREE: MARKETING YOURSELF

Preface

Most students face with great trepidation the prospect of getting a good job following college graduation. Generally, this uncertainty is brought on because students have no idea where they want to go or how to get there. Nonetheless, to succeed in the hunt for great job interviews and the subsequent great jobs they produce, you must know where you are going. It isn't sufficient to say that you want a good job—you must know what type of job you want and where you want it to be located. With these and many other challenges in mind, college students approaching graduation should benefit from *GET THAT INTERVIEW!: The Indispensable Guide for College Grads*, which will help them get where they want to go.

This book is intended solely for college students in the quest for their first job. It is not a reference for any job seeker—their requirements are different. Additionally, the book addresses only students' efforts to obtain job interviews. After that, the variety of situations becomes so enormous that another book is required.

GET THAT INTERVIEW!: The Indispensable Guide for College Grads is a strategy book. It is designed to give you a complete program to meet the challenge of getting great interviews. It shows you how to organize your interview-seeking efforts and develop action plans to carry them out. If you follow the program carefully, you will get the great job interviews that lead to great jobs.

Over the years I have had many meetings with college students who were about to embark on one of the most exciting and frightening experiences of their lifetime—the pursuit of their first full-time job following college graduation. Obtaining a job at any time is difficult, to be sure. But securing a first job is infinitely more daunting than future job searches and thus requires far more preparation and planning to succeed.

Why is getting that first job so difficult? The answer is simple—competition, competition, competition! When colleges disgorge their students each year, over 1.5 million graduates hit the streets at once, each looking for the best (and highest paying) job there is. In addition, many students don't have any idea what kind of work they want to do. And finally, throw into the equation the error-prone efforts students use to seek employment and you have a very difficult scenario to be played out.

There are two reasons why a book on this subject is important. The first is precisely because getting that first job is so difficult; the second because most college seniors are incredibly naive and ill-equipped to tackle the task. After all, some students have never worked, while those who have didn't use the strategies for getting a full-time job when they pursued their part-time or summer employment.

Why should I, an experienced business executive, care about, let alone write a book for, college students pursuing their first gainful employment? Well, initially I didn't care. But over the last few years, many students have come to me for employment advice, and it has occurred to me that I am repeating myself from one meeting to the next. I have also noticed that young people often respect the counsel of a third party over the advice of their own parents—human nature, I suppose. Frankly many parents, through no fault of their own, are ill-equipped to advise their children since they have limited personal experience from which to draw. Finally, the pursuit of good job interviews by college graduates is a subject about which I have found surprisingly little written material.

You may wonder what my credentials are on this subject. After all, it has been some thirty years since I sought my own first job.

You could say I have two stand-up credentials. First and foremost, I have for many years been a hirer of young people. I have seen virtually every application, resume, and interview approach there is. I know what works, what doesn't, and how the job seeker can make things happen. As a matter of fact, I have been hiring people for most of my thirty years in business. I know what I want from an applicant and I believe I know what most other employers are looking for as well.

My second credential for writing this book is the many sessions I have had with college students as they approach the pursuit of their first job. The advice I have given these students is sound and forms the basis for the book.

By definition, you cannot seek more than one first job, so it's very difficult to have broad personal experience. However, I have three children who have graduated from college, and all were quickly successful in getting great first jobs. Utilizing the techniques described in this book, each sought employment in a different profession (commercial real estate, advertising, hotel management), and each had a great number of interviews before a match between company and applicant was made. Of course, each one had different goals and background, but each utilized many aspects of this book, and all three secured excellent positions.

The contents of this book are designed to assist you in the search for your very first job, and the bulk of what follows will be aimed at how you can get many great job interviews. I wish you success with your job seeking and suggest that practicing some (preferably all) of what follows will improve your success in getting the best jobs with the highest financial rewards.

PART ONE

PACKAGING YOUR EXPERIENCE

1. Introduction

Here's the good news—there are a lot of great jobs out there waiting for you! But to get them, you'll have to start working sooner and labor harder and longer than you ever thought necessary. The best positions will be achieved by students who prepare early, pursue all options, utilize all strategies, and expend more energy than their peers. Success awaits those who follow these exhortations.

For the college student approaching graduation, the most important secret for getting a great job is, frankly, getting interviews for those great jobs.

> *Get great job interviews—*
> *it's the only way to get great jobs*

As simple as this sounds, it is a complex and frustrating process that is almost universally poorly done. The likelihood of landing a top job improves infinitely if you have the opportunity to interview for it in the first place. In other words, you can't get a good job if you don't interview for it. In reviewing candidates for a specific position, companies often pore through hundreds of resumes and applications. Naturally, those selected for interviews stand a much greater chance of being hired than those who send in an application but don't get an interview. In the job search, the most important factor in getting a good job is getting good job interviews.

Over the years, students are bombarded by articles in newspapers and magazines outlining the difficulties they face in getting good jobs. During depressed economic times, these articles multiply. And even if the articles are overstatements, they are still depressing. Unfortunately, they are accurate, and that requires college graduates to be smarter candidates and tougher pursuers of jobs.

Despite difficult employment markets, most seniors ultimately find jobs—not necessarily the kind they want and perhaps not at the level of pay they seek. But, for some, a job is a job. This book will provide you with the necessary tools and direction to get great job interviews, which will lead to great jobs with great pay. It can be done. Read on.

Gallia Est . . .

If you have ever taken a course in Latin, you will know what the following sentence—"Gallia est divisa in tres partes"—means: Gaul is divided into three parts. Getting great job interviews has little to do with Latin but a lot to do with parts. In fact, to do an outstanding job of getting great employment interviews, you must pass through "tres partes" (three parts, or stages).

The first part is the "Packaging Your Experience" stage. In this phase you select, from all the experiences you have accumulated since the day you walked into your freshman dorm, those ingredients that will ultimately make up your resume. The second part is the "Preparing for the Interview Search" stage. It includes writing the cover letter and the resume, selecting an employment field of interest, and determining your geographical preference. This step also discusses how to take advantage of your university's career center. The activities in this stage occur during your last year of college. Part three is the "Marketing Yourself" stage, which focuses on the actual strategies you employ to get good interviews. Usually, this step begins in the second semester of your senior year. The best job interviews are obtained if all three steps are taken. If so, good jobs will result.

Six Ingredients

In looking for entry-level employees, companies consider six main ingredients in a student's background.

Six Student Background Ingredients
1. **The college you attended**
2. **Academic achievements**
3. **Courses of study**
4. **Extracurricular activities**
5. **Work experiences**
6. **Unique life experiences**

By the time you read this book, most of these ingredients will have already been established. Other characteristics, such as aptitude and drive, are also considered by employers, but it is difficult to prepare for them in advance.

These six ingredients provide the material for the first stage—

Packaging Your Experiences. This phase simply calls for you to evaluate your employment assets to determine which ones you will stress in your interview search. Note that it is too late at this point to significantly improve your experience characteristics but not too late to decide which ones will serve you best.

For example, employers prefer to interview candidates from the better schools. If you are about to graduate from a *top school*, you will most certainly select that attribute for emphasis. Employers also like to hire the brightest people they can, particularly if the individual's college major matches the job being offered. So, if you have *great grades* or a *pertinent major*, you should stress them.

Employers also look for well-rounded candidates—those with broad college experiences. This means you should emphasize your *extracurricular activities* and related leadership positions. A strong record of *previous business* endeavors is also a characteristic employers seek because, of all your resume assets, this one comes closest to mirroring your future occupation. Certain types of work are more attractive to employers than others and thus should be stressed. Finally, a *unique life experience* can be very attractive to an employer. More on all of this later.

Another major point: In many cases it isn't so much what you've done that catches the eye of the employer, it's how well you've done it. So, in selecting specific characteristics you believe should be emphasized in your interview search, focus on those in which you performed at a level above your peer group.

The Employer's Shoes

Securing an interview, and ultimately succeeding at it, is a selling job. The resume, cover letter, and approach you make to the employer will have a better chance of success if you put yourself in the shoes of the buyer—in this case, the interviewer.

Every type of employment ultimately requires the employee to sell. Of course, salespeople sell all the time, but nonsalespeople sell more often than you think. Almost everyone in business "sells" their ideas whether they are as big as the need to pursue an acquisition of another company or as small as the way a set of figures should be arranged on a report for the boss. Perhaps the single most important ingredient in business success is the ability to sell.

And the most important part of selling is the need to put the "seller" in the place of the "buyer." In other words, in order to sell successfully (ideas, products, or yourself as a possible employee), you must put yourself in the position of the person to whom you are trying to sell. Until you can "see the sale" from the buyer's point of view, you will not succeed as a "salesperson." This is true throughout life, and it is especially true of the job interviewing process. Attempt to see the job search through the eyes of the interviewer, and your chances for the interview will improve significantly.

The importance of this point cannot be overemphasized. It came home to me vividly a short while ago when a young woman was applying for a position with a major financial firm. She had gone through several interviews and meetings with the firm's local management. At each step of the way, she was successful enough to advance to the next stage. Finally, her last interview was imminent—it was with the regional director of the company in Los Angeles.

The young woman called me before the interview and asked a simple question. She said, "Please give me some 'regional' questions to ask." She had recognized the need to talk with the regional director on his level, not on her level. In effect, she wanted to put herself in the position of the regional director and spend part of the meeting interviewing the regional director. The director was impressed and the young woman got the job.

This story emphasizes the importance of looking at the interview search through the eyes of the interviewer. When selecting your most favorable assets to project, select them as if you were the employer. What is it you think the employer would be most interested in learning about you? When you approach companies, think how you would like to be approached if you were the hirer. The better able you are to "sit in the chair of the interviewer," the greater your successes will be.

Let's now turn our attention to emphasizing your college experiences to see how they can help you stand out in the crowd of competition.

2. College Attended

Before we begin, let me point out that it is highly unlikely any college graduate will excel in all six experience categories mentioned in the previous chapter. Some won't excel in any. This is the primary reason why you need to evaluate your assets so that you can focus on your standout characteristics. Let's start off with a discussion of the school you are attending.

This may be the most controversial section of the book, because it will appear to denigrate many fine colleges and universities in our country. An outstanding education and a good job following graduation can be acquired from almost any undergraduate school in our nation. As a matter of fact, the old saying, "You get out of something exactly what you put into it," applies here.

Nonetheless, there is absolutely no question in my mind, and in the minds of most other employers, that the school from which a candidate graduates has a great influence in getting great job interviews. If this book is to enhance your ability to obtain job interviews with top companies for top positions, then it must address the subject of which school you will be graduating from.

> *The school from which you graduate*
> *is a big factor for prospective interviewers.*

Having stated the premise, we have also delivered the message. For the sake of example only, I will use Harvard as representative of top U.S. colleges academically. No, I did not attend Harvard. In fact, I graduated from one of its chief rivals. But in the business world, Harvard is considered by many to be number one, just as M.I.T. and California Tech are considered tops in the engineering community. To avoid naming an institution with a less highly regarded reputation, I will make up a school to represent the contrast from Harvard. Let's call it Northern University College. Through all my research, I have not found a school named Northern University College, so I believe the name is fictitious.

Harvard or Northern University College?

Now, if you were an employer faced with the decision to interview either a Harvard or a Northern University College graduate (assuming they are equal in all other regards), I submit you would select the applicant from Harvard over the one from Northern University College. Perhaps this is unfair. But if employers are looking for the best candidates to interview, why wouldn't they elect to interview individuals who were accepted at and will graduate from the toughest schools?

The Top Schools

Top Schools - By Reputation
Top Schools - In Your Field
Top Schools - Where You Plan to Work

Of course, by the time you read this, it will be too late to change your college institution. But it will not be too late to decide whether you should emphasize your school in your interview-seeking steps.

Interestingly enough, though, the subject goes deeper. The better a school's reputation in a specific discipline, the more likely its graduates will be interviewed by top employers in related fields. Not everyone can go to or graduate from Harvard, nor do all want to because Harvard is not number one in all fields. For example, Cal Tech graduates outstanding engineers, Texas A&M top agricultural students, and Cornell excellent hotel management people. But graduating from a top school in your field will significantly improve your chances of getting interviews with the top organizations in those specialties. If this applies to you, then you should stress this asset.

Local Phenomenon

There is still another consideration. Employers in some cities lean toward candidates from local universities. This is true in many locations and, for example, it is certainly true in Dallas, Texas. There, the business community believes the leading school is Southern Methodist University (SMU), a college that historically has supplied many Dallas business leaders. SMU is well thought of throughout the Dallas business community, and as such adds credibility to SMU graduates seeking employment in Dallas.

While you might scoff at the phenomenon of local preference, we find it's true in many locations throughout the country. It is just natural for people to be proud of their local university.

If you are graduating from a school in a community where you will be seeking work, you have several additional advantages. The first is in networking. Graduates of the same school tend to be more helpful to each other than to graduates of other schools. In Dallas, many SMU businesspeople are active in the community. They often refer SMU graduates to known job opportunities. A second reason is that many local interviewers have also graduated from the same local school. They obviously think well of their school and should feel equally positive when interviewing a recent graduate of that school.

Third, you can make a number of business connections with alumni who participate in local university activities—such as alumni programs, great lecture series, fundraising, and so on. These contacts, helpful upon graduation, can be invaluable in future years.

While graduating from a top school is a big asset, graduating from a top college in your specialty is equally beneficial. And, of course, graduating from a well-thought-of local school can be a big plus as well. If your college qualifies in any of these categories, you have a leg up on your competition, and you should stress this connection in seeking great job interviews.

3. Courses of Study

Let's understand one thing first. In academics, there are really two considerations—grades and courses of study. We will deal with grades in the next chapter, but let's look first at your course emphasis.

Most students will be well into their major before they read this book. Majors are usually picked in the sophomore year, and by the time you begin to look for job interviews, it will be difficult, if not impossible, to change your area of concentration.

Your Major and Your Job

You will present to an employer the best possible impression if your major matches the job you are seeking. For instance, if your major is accounting and you apply for a job at an accounting firm, there are at least two reasons why you will have a better chance of getting an interview than, for example, someone who majored in marketing. Your accounting major obviously gave you better training for accounting work than did the marketing major's training. And, because you have shown an interest in accounting since your early college days (when you selected accounting as a major), and you are still interested enough to pursue accounting as a career, you are more likely to become a long-term employee for a CPA firm. The odds are less that a marketing major would enjoy accounting over the long term. As a matter of fact, the marketing major probably wouldn't stand a chance of getting an interview at an accounting firm anyway.

> *You will be ahead of your competition*
> *if your major corresponds with the job you seek.*

The relationship between your college major and the type of job you seek is very important—the closer the match, the greater the resume asset. Sometimes, however, there is no correlation between a student's major and job preference. For instance, I heard recently of a college graduate who applied for a position as a stockbroker. His college major, it turned out, was advertising. In this case, though he majored in advertising, the applicant did not seek a job in the advertising business. The perceptive employer had to ask the question, "Why did you spend four years pursuing a specialized major if you had no intention of seeking a career in that business?" Small wonder that the individual was still seeking employment eight months after graduation. From the same school in the same year, my second son graduated with the same advertising degree but had no interest in seeking employment in any other field. He obtained an advertising position promptly.

Alternative Solutions

If you are fortunate enough to have your major and your desired career field match, good for you. But, if not, what do you do then? Happily, there are several solutions you can consider. The first is to find a common functional thread between the position you are seeking and your college major. For example, if you have an advertising major but desire to work in the petroleum industry, perhaps there is a position at a petroleum firm that would incorporate subjects from your major. This blend would allow you to utilize some of your advertising skills while still meeting your desire to work in the energy field.

If you still have some college time left, another method of matching your major to a different business is to alter your course load to have a double major. This will provide you with greatly enhanced flexibility when it comes time for interviews. Even in your senior year, you might be able to replace an elective course or two with courses that could result in a minor along with your major. Any time prospective employers see two majors (or a major and a minor), they are likely to be impressed both with your academic effort and with your breadth of experience, and your chances of getting great interviews will increase. If you have a double major or a major and a minor, you should stress this as you seek interviews.

A very specific major (statistics, for example) allows little latitude in the interview search but a more general major has expansion possibilities. Examples of a broader major would be business or liberal arts. A business degree can be a plus when seeking a position with a bank but a statistics degree might not. Stressing your major in broad terms can widen your interview prospects.

If you find that your major and job preference don't match, consider changing your major to the desired field. If this decision must be made late in your college career, you will have to extend your time in school to a fifth year at significant additional cost to you or your parents. It will also raise questions with employers as to why it took you five years to graduate. Still, staying for the fifth year might be the right choice.

Finally, of course, if your major and job preference aren't even close, graduate school instead of the job market might be appropriate. With this course of action, you can major in your desired field in graduate school, thereby bringing your job preference and major into line.

Your major is vitally important in securing great job interviews. It is hoped your major relates directly to the job you will be seeking. Keep in mind that the goal of this book is to get you job interviews, and employers are far more likely to grant you an interview if the job you're seeking matches your college major.

4. Academic Achievement

Now that we have determined how important the college major is, let's turn our attention to academic achievement, sometimes referred to as marks or grade point average. Interestingly, while grades are critical in seeking the first job, they have considerably less impact when you pursue future positions. Though I have changed jobs occasionally, no one, except in my initial interviews, has ever asked me what my college marks were. But they did when I pursued my first job.

In fact, once you are beyond your first position, the most important college asset you will have is not your course of study or your marks, but the school from which you graduated. Business employers in the future will be impressed if you graduated from Harvard or the Wharton School, even if you were at the bottom of your class (which they won't know or even ask about). Later employers will be less impressed if you graduated from a school with a lesser reputation, even if you ranked near the top of your class academically. By the time you are in your thirties, employers are more interested in your work accomplishments than your academic record.

> *Emphasize your academic successes—they are the most important ingredients you have.*

However, academic accomplishment is the most important asset you can present in your initial employment efforts. It is one of the few characteristics an employer can clearly measure. While most other resume ingredients are not easily evaluated, academic achievement is.

Top Grades

Perhaps it is too simple to say that the higher your marks are at graduation, the greater your chances of getting interviews with top companies. Nonetheless, in most cases, the employer is looking for bright candidates and more likely will grant interviews to prospective employees who show top grades.

Yet good grades are not a guarantee of success. Recently, a business friend complained to me about all the bright young people at his firm—none of whom, he contended, could communicate. Brains (defined here as top grades) are great, but if you can't describe, sell, or otherwise communicate ideas and suggestions to your bosses and peers, what good are your high marks? Despite my associate's concerns, grades are vital when pursuing top job interviews. They allow the candidate to stand out in a crowd of job applicants, and that enhances the individual's chance of getting interviews. Good marks are also important because, to a potential employer, they are one of the few accurate measures of your capabilities.

The subject of marks should also be addressed from another perspective. Let's say in your freshman and sophomore years, you were a C student. Along the way, you learned the value of good grades, so you turned on the afterburners, worked hard, and improved your grades to a B minus average, a commendable effort with excellent results. Contrast that with a classmate who is very bright and would normally have an A average. However, for this student, college is an exciting, activity-filled environment, and our A potential student devoted some of her time to nonacademic pursuits. As a result her overall grade level slipped to a B plus.

Now as a prospective employer, you have two candidates, one with a B plus average, the other with a B minus average. Which one does the employer select for an interview if he can only pick one? Probably the B plus average student if all other characteristics are similar. But in this case the employer could be wrong. Perhaps the better student to interview would be you, the B minus student, because you recognized the task at hand, went to work, and made significant gains. Your classmate spent more time having fun. Your overall improvement could be a great asset to stress to potential interviewers.

Grade Point Averages

There are three grade point averages (GPAs) that are part of your record. The first is your overall GPA through your complete college career. The second is the GPA for your major and the third is your junior and senior years' GPA. Employers like to focus on your overall GPA first, the GPA for your major second, and your final two-year GPA third.

Grade Point Average—A Powerful Ally		
Title	Type	Quality
Overall GPA	Four-Year GPA	Strongest Suit
Major GPA	GPA with Major Subjects	Strong Positive
Later Years GPA	Junior/Senior-Year GPA	Plus Asset

Despite employers' preferences, the decision on which GPA to stress in your interview search is easy—you cite the best (highest) GPA of the three. If the GPA for your last two years is the highest, that's the one you should promote. If it is your overall GPA, focus on it. Emphasize your strongest GPA!

The bottom line here is simple—if your marks are good, they will help you get great job interviews. If your grade point average is 3.5 or above, it should be heavily stressed. If it is between 3.0 and 3.5, it can be valuable unless the position being sought requires a very high grade point average. If your average is below 3.0, the subject of marks should be avoided by the applicant. You have no obligation to offer your marks to an employer unless asked.

While grades and grade point averages are the most measurable scholastic characteristic, academic achievement awards and honors carry very heavy weight with employers. Many colleges extend awards for achievement in specific courses and majors. Sometimes these awards come with material benefits.

If, for example, you are a sociology major and were selected by the sociology department staff at your school as the top student in the department—thereby winning the Robert B. Harris Sociology Award—your qualifications will be greatly enhanced. These awards are usually given with an eye on both the student's grades in the specific major and other, less tangible accomplishments such as most improvement, best thesis, and most innovative. Remembering that your job is selling yourself, what better asset is there than an academic honor or award presented to the student by the faculty? Stress this.

The combination of high grades and academic honors is powerful—stronger perhaps than any other applicant's characteristics. Together, they will project a positive image of you to employers.

5. Extracurricular Activities

When I was an undergraduate, I recognized very early that I would benefit significantly if I had a broad resume—one that would include accomplishments beyond just marks. As a result, I became very busy "on campus" participating in many activities and achieving several major leadership roles. In fact, in my senior year, I was selected one of the school's ten top seniors based primarily on my extracurricular activities. I was also selected for membership in my school's junior and senior honor societies. During my interview search, I had many interviews, in part, I am sure, because of my breadth of activities and related leadership roles.

The success achieved in academics is the most critical aspect of the passage through college. But, as we have noted, it is not the only quality sought by prospective employers. Indeed, for some positions, academic achievement is less important than other characteristics a candidate can offer.

Well-Roundedness

How is it possible that a candidate's other characteristics are more important than high grades? Aren't all companies seeking the brightest students? Many of them are, of course. But many companies want "well-rounded" candidates—applicants with broad college experience. Well-roundedness can be the result of any number of things—extracurricular activities, travel, unique experiences, employment history, community involvement, leadership, and so on. Many companies prefer this type of individual because they offer jobs that either require people skills or have broad responsibilities.

People-skills jobs are those that require an ability to relate to and work with a wide assortment of people—company employees and/or individuals outside the company. Skills that are most effective in these environments often come from nonacademic pursuits. Sales, for example, is the quintessential people-skills position. In addition, companies have a variety of other positions calling for people with broad experiences. Many companies, for instance, offer long training programs—up to two years. Candidates with varied backgrounds often fit well into these positions. There are many other examples.

Perhaps the most effective way to establish your credentials as a well-rounded candidate is through your participation in college extracurricular activities. In leafing through any college yearbook, you will find an enormous number of committees and activities available to students. The list of organizations that exist at most schools seems endless.

However, the discussion of what a well-rounded student is has just begun—in fact, the easiest part is behind us. We know that extracurricular activities are important and that there are many activities that can fill the bill, but the most valuable aspects of extracurricular activities are still to come.

One of the things employers take into consideration when evaluating your extracurricular record is which of the organizations you have joined bear some relationship to the type of career you are pursuing. Although many college activities have little connection to the job market, some do. Most majors, for instance, have a club—the marketing club, the Spanish club, the engineering club, and so on. Those and others, such as the college newspaper staff, dormitory advisor, college greeter, could look good to interviewers because they will see that you devoted some of your free time to activities that have some relationship to your future career, further underscoring the commitment you have made to your chosen profession. In your interview search, you should stress activities that relate to your job preference.

Leadership

To present a well-rounded picture, participation in college activities is a big asset. However, employers are interested in more than just your involvement in a club, group, or committee. They want to see how well you did in those organizations. This element is universally measured by the leadership positions you have held. Generally, students perform best in activities they like best, and usually those who are active in a group have a much better chance of becoming its leader. Employers want to see leadership roles if they are seeking well-rounded applicants.

> *Stress your college leadership*
> *roles in the interview search.*

Most leadership positions in college organizations are earned through efforts you made during your initial years of school (freshman-junior) and are reached in the senior year. If you have obtained leadership roles in extracurricular activities by building on your earlier years, you will have excellent assets to show prospective interviewers.

A perfect example is the young man I know who participated in only one campus activity. He decided he would be active in his college fraternity. In his sophomore year, he held two positions—party chairman and intramural chairman. In his junior year, he became fraternity secretary and newsletter chairman. In the first semester of his senior

> **"In retailing, it's location, location, location! In extracurricular activities, it's leadership, leadership, leadership!"**

year, he was the pledge trainer. To say this young man was active in his fraternity is an understatement. As far as a prospective employer was concerned, however, this young man, well-rounded though he may have been, did not show significant leadership credentials. How is it that he could be so active in his fraternity and not be elected president?

The young man came to me and said several fraternity members had approached him about running for president for the second semester of senior year. He was reluctant to do so because of the work involved and because the position would cover the last semester of his senior year when he wanted to spend his time seeking employment. My advice to him was most emphatic. Run for president! If you lose the election, you will be no worse off than if you didn't run, at least as it relates to your employment credentials. But if you win, the achievement would stand out with gold stars. Incidentally, he did run for president, he did win the election, and he did secure a fine job.

Another young man came to me in his junior year and solicited my thoughts on how he could advance his job-seeking effort, which was to begin the following year. I gave him the leadership idea and he took it, as shown in an excerpt from a letter he sent me from school several months later—"I took your advice about being a leader of a group and have been chosen as chairman of my school's law committee. Although I am in fact at the moment the only active member of the group . . ." Small wonder he is chairman of the group! More important, however, he created an organization and became its first leader. Where there's a will, there's a way.

Awards and Honors

As in academics, rewards and honors are prevalent in extracurricular activities. Many schools, for instance, have honor societies for excellence in campus activities. As indicated earlier, my university has a junior honor society and three senior societies. Membership is based on outstanding participation in college activities, and election to membership is extremely competitive. Acceptance into these honor societies says a lot about the individual—peer recognition—and the interviewer will be impressed.

Many athletic teams have multiple awards and honors at year's end—most valuable player, most improved player, newcomer of the year, team spirit leader, and so on. Athletic conferences also bestow awards and honors. Fraternities and sororities single out members who make the biggest contribution during the year. My university selects four seniors each year (based on nonacademic achievement) for prestigious awards, and it also invites two seniors to serve on its board of trustees for a term.

If you have been selected for recognition by a certified college group—academic, athletic, extracurricular—you have an enormous advantage over your competition for great job interviews. Any recognition from these groups should be stressed when seeking interviews.

Employers are looking for many characteristics, but if I had to choose just two, they would be high academic accomplishment and leadership traits. In my role as a hirer of young people, the trait I look for the most in an applicant is the success the individual has had over time. If the candidate has a pattern of success in his early years, he will probably continue to be successful. Success in academics is measured by the student's grades, while success in nonacademic pursuits is measured by leadership roles. Hopefully, you have spent time in activities where you achieved a leadership position so that these can be included on your list of assets.

If you think about it, it's very simple. Employers are looking for the best people they can find for their company. What better measure of being the best is there than having your peer group vote you into a prestigious position? This is the ultimate recognition—people you live, work, and play with every day singling you out as a leader. That's what the employer wants to know.

6. Work Experience

In an attempt to project an irresistible candidate, we have concentrated on academics and extracurricular activities, both directly associated with college. Combined, these areas complete a major portion of a job seeker's credentials. The next piece of the puzzle is your work experience.

Many college graduates obtain permanent employment positions without any significant prior work experience. But those who have reasonably important, related business experience to their credit have a major advantage over other job seekers.

> *Those who have business experience similar*
> *to the job being sought have a major edge.*

There are several tiers of work experience a job candidate can have, and certainly the highest tier leads to better interviewing opportunities. College graduates with no work experience can get interviews, but can you imagine them getting the best jobs with the highest compensation? Not likely. The interviewer will say to herself, "The candidate has never worked, let alone lived the nine-to-five regimen—how is he going to relate to the discipline of a regular job? And, what about his ambition level?" Under the best of circumstances, it would be a difficult adjustment. The employer will often look elsewhere.

M.W.E.

There are three different levels of employment experience a college student can have. The first, and least attractive to potential employers, is Miscellaneous Work Experience (M.W.E.). Examples are babysitting, lifeguarding, and lawncutting. The drawbacks of this type of work—work that is generally done alone—are that it is difficult to verify by an employer, it provides no assurance that the work was done regularly, assessing the quality of the work performance is difficult, and in most cases the work requires minimum mental effort. Finally, it is not conducted in a normal business environment, thus providing no opportunity for the candidate to experience the daily routine of a repetitive business day.

Levels of Work Experience

M.W.E. - Miscellaneous Work Experience
N.E.E. - Normal Employment Experience
S.W.E. - Similar Work Experience

Let's distinguish at this point between a job that looks good to an interviewer and one that pays well. Just because an individual earns a lot of money in summer work does not prima facie make it a good asset in the interview search. For instance, properly organized, a person who earns money by cutting lawns can cut three lawns a day (at, say, $20 a lawn). A lawncutter working a full day can bring in $300 a week. If he cuts lawns for the summer, he could earn up to $3,000; if he started in April and went through October, he might earn $7,000. Despite these high earnings, the job may not necessarily be an employment asset. However, if he can document that his lawncutting activities were performed by a company he organized and ran, which included additional employees, and were not just a job, his appeal to employers is improved.

N.E.E.

Normal Employment Experience (N.E.E.) is the next tier of business experience for the student. Generally, this type of work is with a company, but it is not usually mind-expanding. Examples of this would be a position in a retail store as a sales clerk, serving as a delivery person, and employment in an office environment doing repetitive tasks. These positions are characterized by little training, limited thinking on the part of the job holder, and few challenges. Nonetheless, this work does have the advantage of fitting the student into a business-type atmosphere, has some mental challenges, and can show a candidate's adaptability to the work environment.

S.W.E.

However, to obtain a top job with top pay after graduation, you should have work experience on the third level—Similar Work Experience (S.W.E.). At this level, your employment experience should be in environments similar to those you are seeking at graduation. These will generally be in businesses where you undertook challenging, important functions.

Picture yourself as an employer planning to hire a top candidate for your company. Assuming all else is equal, would you pick the candidate whose summers were spent as a sales clerk in a department store or the one who spent summers working in the same business and function in which she now is seeking full-time employment? Chances are you'd prefer the candidate with similar work experiences. This is the best type of work experience for the college student, and if you have it, you should emphasize it during your search for great job interviews.

Let's say, for example, that you want to become a stockbroker upon graduation. Your prior work as a camp counselor wouldn't be much of an asset, but work in a brokerage office would. And it would be even better if you had spent the summer as a "caller" in the brokerage office. A caller helps registered brokers make prospecting calls. If your plans are to become an architect, what better job experience could you have had than working at an architectural firm? Suppose you want to become an accountant after graduation. Your best foot forward, at least as far as your credentials are concerned, is related work experience at a CPA firm.

Once again, put yourself in the position of the employer. Don't you agree that you would be best served in your quest for a top job if you have serious, related work experience for the position being sought? The greater the similarity between the job being pursued and work performed during college, the better your chance of getting the desired interview.

Internship

We now know that, if you want the best job you can get, you should stress your summer work experiences of the type described in tier three—work related to your career choice. Perhaps, instead of gainful employment, you had a summer internship. This is a position with a bona-fide corporation that may provide little financial compensation but that offers great opportunity to learn first hand about a specific business.

This type of experience is also appealing to employers because it could indicate significant involvement in a related business. If the position is unpaid (as some of them are), you can turn it into a great plus. If an individual has summer experience in a related activity and did it for nothing, what greater commitment can a candidate make to a specific career field? The interviewer will be impressed.

The next consideration to be made about work experience concerns the regularity of work performed. Most employers would like to see employment activities every summer during the college years. Interviewers get very uneasy when they see one (or more) summers without work experience. There are, of course, many good reasons why a student doesn't work during a summer, but be prepared to defend yourself when the interviewer asks you what you did during the summer between your freshman and sophomore years. If it appears you wasted the summer (define that as goofing off), you've lost ground.

If you really want to impress an employer, you should show work experience each summer during your college career and should further show that the responsibilities of that work increased each year. It doesn't have to be with the same company each year, but the strongest impression is made when an applicant's duties expand from year to year. Suppose you were a department store sales clerk in your first summer. The next summer's work could be the same function in a much larger department. The following summer you worked in the accounting office of another department store, and the last summer you were made an assistant buyer in women's wear. That's increasing responsibility and increasing challenges. It will be a big asset in your search for great job interviews in the retail business.

In conclusion, employment experience is a very important part of a job seeker's assets. Remember, the more relevant your summer work is to the type of job you hope to get after college, the better your chances are of getting great interviews.

7. Unique Life Experience

The sixth and last potential ingredient of any outstanding candidate is your unique life experiences. Having a unique life experience is an enormous asset—one that can quickly make your credentials stand out from the competition. What is a unique life experience? It is something significant that you have accomplished outside the normal routine and is something few people achieve.

Does getting straight A's in college qualify as a unique life experience? No. Does being captain of your university's football team fit the description? No. Does being president of your college senior class qualify? No. True, these are outstanding achievements that have desirable characteristics, but they don't qualify as a unique life experience because they were achieved within the framework of your normal activities—attending college.

What Is It?

A unique life experience is normally something accomplished outside your daily world—something that most students would not even be exposed to. Perhaps the best way to define a unique life experience is through the use of examples:

1. There are very few activities you can participate in before college that would qualify as a unique life experience. However, one would be earning the Eagle Scout award or the Girl Scout Gold award. Each fits the description of a unique life experience because it was accomplished outside your day-to-day activities and is something rarely achieved. Becoming an Eagle Scout or Gold award winner is one of the few unique life experiences that can be gained prior to college.

2. Working as a page in your state senate or house of representatives would be a unique life experience. In addition to the uniqueness of the position, the contacts you might make in that environment can be enormously valuable in later years.

3. Another unique life experience would be holding elective office in a city or town government. Every once in a while you hear of a

college student who is active in local government and who gets elected to a city position. It doesn't have to be an important post—just the experience of campaigning and serving is a powerful asset.

4. Certain types of international travel can be considered unique life experiences. You need to be careful about this because overseas experiences per se are no longer unique. Their uniqueness would depend on location (the Far East is unique, Europe is not), reason for being there (working your way through Europe for a summer is more likely to qualify as a unique life experience than is a two-week vacation there financed by your parents), or activity pursued (living with a foreign family is more unique than doing the grand tour).

5. Attending a major European university for a year qualifies as a unique life experience. This type of educational opportunity can be arranged in conjunction with your college academic program. To have the experience of living in a foreign culture for several months or a year adds an intriguing element to your resume, not to mention expanding your language skills.

6. Performing social work in a foreign land also qualifies as a unique life experience. The Peace Corps is an obvious example. Church witness programs, which are programs where students promote their personal religion, would also be appropriate.

7. Creating and building a viable business during college is a very attractive unique life experience. Every school has a handful of students who spend their nonacademic hours in business pursuits. A few even develop a profitable company complete with products, employees, P&L statements, and facilities. At graduation, employers are looking for people who will be successful in the business world. What better credentials could you have for an important job than experience in running your own company?

If you free your imagination, you will think of many more unique life experiences. As you review your accomplishments, see if you can identify one (or more) in your life that qualifies. In fact, there may still be time before you begin the interview search to participate in an activity that could qualify as a unique life experience.

> *A unique life experience can vault your*
> *application beyond many of your competitors.*

Your unique life experience alone, if it stands out, could set your application apart from all the others. A unique life experience can never be a disadvantage if it is properly marketed by you. It can also offset an otherwise average resume. If you have a unique life experience, stress it in your interview search.

8. Experience Rater

So now you have the six major ingredients of a great applicant—the college you attended, your courses of study, academic achievement, extracurricular activities, work experience, and, possibly, a unique life experience. The purpose of this chapter is to give you a method of measuring your college credentials. Most undergraduates have no way of knowing if they are a strong candidate or a weak one. What follows here is a relatively easy way for you to rate your background.

On page 30 is a blank form you can complete yourself. It is called an Experience Rater and can be used any time during your college life. It assigns point credits for various levels of accomplishment in each experience category. In most cases, the top rating in each group receives five points credit for superior accomplishment, three points for coming close, and one point for average results. While this is a somewhat simplistic approach, students who want insight on how they stack up will find that the Experience Rater is an accurate measuring tool. In time you will also find that recruiters use a measuring tool similar to the Experience Rater in their initial evaluation process. In many ways, the quality of a candidate is subjective, but the Experience Rater will provide some guidance. It might be helpful to review the previous chapters as you complete your Experience Rater.

How to Score

How do you rate your college credentials? Beyond the grade point average, few students really know how well they have done at college, and they have even less awareness of how their successes measure up against competition from throughout the country. The Experience Rater will help. Let's start with the *college you attend*. The chapter on college attended stated that you will stand a better chance of getting great job interviews if you graduate from one of the top universities in the country.

For example, if you will graduate from, say, an Ivy League school or a Duke, Northwestern, or Stanford, award yourself five points for this category. These schools are considered among the best in many disciplines. If you are to graduate from the next tier of colleges, give yourself three points. Many other schools deserve one point, though I should make the point that there are a handful of schools (Northern University College perhaps?) that add virtually no credibility to a candidacy and might not warrant even one point. Further, give yourself a higher rating if the school you will be graduating from is among the top schools in your particular field of professional interest or if it is a university located in the city in which you expect to work.

In this discussion we are not trying to rate a university's educational qualities nor discourage students who don't attend top-rated schools. We are just trying to point out the importance of how schools are perceived in the eyes of potential interviewers. School ratings can change over time and, of course, everyone is entitled to their own opinion on how a college is rated. The schools mentioned above have, for decades, been rated well and are presented only as examples of the top-rated schools.

I would also hasten to add, however, that students are not generally good judges of the quality and reputation of their own schools. Very few undergraduates think poorly of their school, so their judgment can be cloudy. If you are not sure how your college is rated by employers, go to others for guidance.

The second ingredient in a good candidacy is the *course of study* (major) you are pursuing. Award a rating of five points if the job you seek at graduation is exactly in line with your college major. For example, if you are seeking an accounting degree, give yourself five Experience Rater points if you are applying for a job in accounting.

However, if you are a public relations major, you would rate just three points if you decide to pursue a position in sales. The public relations major is in some ways similar to the type of work you are seeking, but it is not an absolute match. Virtually anyone who graduates should award himself at least one point for completing the requirements in any major even if it does not come close to matching the career path. Thus, even though you are a history major, you should credit yourself with one point even if your job-seeking efforts are, for example, in the communications industry.

Interviewers are often skeptical of students who complete a four-year undergraduate program in four and a half, five, or more years. There are, of course, mitigating factors that can cause students to take longer than the prescribed time to graduate. However, if there is no valid justification for extending your time in school beyond four years, such as a student who must work to go to college, *deduct* one point on the Experience Rater.

Many college students believe that it is acceptable to take five years to complete undergraduate school. This attitude may have been approved or fostered by the student's parents who suggested a slower path through college so that the college years can be better enjoyed. To an interviewer, it smacks of laziness and lack of purpose. College is expensive both in terms of time and money, and to squander both for a little lighter schedule is not the way to get the interviewer's attention.

The easiest credential to measure is *academic achievement.* When interviewers ask you what your grade point average is, they will receive a specific number and will make judgments from that answer. Remember, use the highest GPA you have from the three choices (four-year GPA, major GPA, or last two years GPA). For guidance purposes, here are the Experience Rater point values for your best grade point average:

Grade Point Average	Experience Rater Points
3.5–4.0	5
3.0–3.5	3
2.5–3.0	1
Under 2.5	0

You should give yourself one additional point if you have been the recipient of one or more academic honors or awards during your undergraduate days.

Less easy to evaluate are your *extracurricular activities.* In this category, leadership is what distinguishes five-point ratings from the others. If you have held positions of leadership, give yourself five points. Examples are class president, fraternity president, captain of an athletic team, president of the interfraternity council, editor of the yearbook or school newspaper, and so on. These are top positions to which your peer group elected you and for which you should receive top rating points.

Lesser positions in school activities (such as vice president, associate editor) and/or participation in a large number of activities without leadership roles earns you three points in the Experience Rater. If you participated in just a few activities and held no responsible positions, you can credit yourself with just one point. Those who did not participate in any extracurricular activity deserve no points. As with academic achievement, give yourself one additional point if you received an extracurricular activity honor or award.

The next experience ingredient is summer and school *employment.* This category can be enormously helpful in seeking top interviews even if your college credentials are average in other respects.

Award yourself five points only if you have career-related, business-type jobs during college. This could be either summer work in an industry similar to your permanent job search or in functional work related to the type of work you will seek at graduation. A summer selling job would be appropriate, for example, if you were looking for a full-time position in sales.

Clerking in a department store is an obvious function that would qualify for three points. Receptionist-related activities would also fit this category. Such activities as waitressing, lifeguarding, long-term babysitting, lawn work, and so on, would warrant one point. Those who didn't work during the summer or the school year should receive no points.

A *unique life experience* is the last experience ingredient to evaluate. In many cases, determining whether you have a unique life experience is a judgment call. Use the examples in Chapter 7 as a guide.

Of the six key ingredients, the unique life experience category is the only one that doesn't warrant the five-three-one point scale. The reason is simple—you either have a unique life experience or you don't. You can't have a partially unique experience—it's either unique or it isn't.

If you believe you have a unique life experience, award yourself five points. If you don't have one, give yourself no points.

Although completing the Experience Rater is a relatively easy process, remember our goal is to determine how strong your candidacy is and, through this process, to find out what your potential is for securing interviews with top employers. Prospective employers want to hire the best candidates they can. Consequently, they are looking for undergraduates who:

1. Are graduating from the best schools,
2. Are pursuing employment related to their major,
3. Have achieved high academic results,
4. Have shown significant leadership positions,
5. Have had attractive work experience, and
6. Have a unique life experience.

To score five points in each of the six basic ingredients is highly unlikely. Do not be discouraged if your rating in all categories is not the highest. Needless to say, few can do it all—even the top ones. I have seen students get fine interviews scoring five points in only one of the six categories.

THE COLLEGE STUDENT'S
EXPERIENCE RATER

	Your Rating (Check One)	Point Score	Your Points
1. College Attended			
a. Top university		5	
b. Good college		3	
c. All others		1	
Your Point Total			
2. Course of Study			
a. Major same as position sought		5	
b. Major similar to position sought		3	
c. All other majors		1	
d. Over four years to graduate		–1	
Your Point Total			
3. Academic Achievement			
a. 3.5–4.0 grade point average		5	
b. 3.0–3.4 grade point average		3	
c. 2.5–2.9 grade point average		1	
d. Under 2.5 grade point average		0	
e. Academic honor credit		1	
Your Point Total			
4. Extracurricular Activities			
a. Major leadership positions		5	
b. Participated in many activities		3	
c. Limited activity participation		1	
d. No activities		0	
e. Extracurricular honor credit		1	
Your Point Total			
5. Work Experience			
a. Directly related to position sought		5	
b. Unrelated business employment		3	
c. Miscellaneous work experience		1	
d. No work experience		0	
Your Point Total			
6. Unique Life Experience			
a. Unique life experience		5	
b. No unique life experience		0	
Your Point Total			
YOUR EXPERIENCE RATER POINT TOTAL			

What Does It Mean?

When the ratings are tallied, what do the results mean? Needless to say, the higher the overall rating, the greater your chance is of getting interviews for top positions with outstanding future opportunities and attractive compensation.

For guidance purposes, a student who scores 19 points or more on the Experience Rater is a candidate for top interviews upon graduation. To accomplish this, in most cases you will have to excel in at least two of the six ingredients. The following will give you some idea of the quality of your candidacy and thus the type of opportunity you would most likely qualify for:

Total Experience Rater Points	Experience Quality
19–up	Outstanding
17–18	Very Good
15–16	Good
10–14	Fair
0–9	Poor

Understand this additional point: While a strong background can enhance your ability to get great job interviews, a good interview, test-taking, and follow-up meetings can improve your chances of getting a great job. In other words, the Experience Rater is designed only to give you an idea what level of job you can anticipate getting an interview for, not whether other factors can improve upon (or detract from) your success in getting a job after the interview is secured.

Students who are good interviewers have a significantly higher chance of getting better jobs. Conversely, students who perform poorly on a company aptitude test reduce their chances. The point here is that the Experience Rater does not decide the job you will get, only the importance of the job for which you should be able to secure interviews.

Using the discussion in this chapter as a basis, determine your rating in each of the six key ingredients in the Experience Rater. Honestly evaluate your credentials, then insert your ratings. When you have added the related points, you will learn how you score on the Experience Rater and for what level of job opportunity you could expect to secure interviews. You will find in Chapter 13 a fictitious resume constructed to depict a strongly experienced student. It is then measured on the Experience Rater for evaluation. Compare it with yours.

PART TWO

PREPARING FOR THE INTERVIEW SEARCH

9. Introduction

Now that you have identified your most attractive credentials, it's time to move to the second of the three major stages in obtaining great job interviews—preparation for the interview search. This stage includes activities that should be addressed and completed before you actually enter the job market. All of them should be undertaken in the first semester of your senior year so that the second semester can be devoted entirely to your primary mission of getting great job interviews.

Several considerations need to be addressed during this phase, including the most important ones—what kind of work do you want to do and where do you want to do it?

> *Significant preparation prior to the*
> *interview search greatly improves your chances.*

Needless to say, before the job search begins, you need to know where you're going. Also during this period (sooner if possible), you should become acquainted with your university's career center. There is plenty to be gained by joining forces with that organization. And, of course, you need to understand the importance of the resume and then write it. Finally, you need to create and write the companion piece to the resume—the cover letter—before seeking job interviews.

In your preparation activities, it might be helpful to follow the Senior Year Timetable—Fall Semester (below). This provides you with a guide to the timing of the interview search preparation steps. While the dates on the timetable are strongly suggested, modifications to fit your school's schedule are acceptable.

Table 9.1   SENIOR YEAR TIME TABLE—Fall Semester

Date	Activities
September/October	Visit your school's career center to determine what programs, activities, resources, and interviews will be available during the year and when they are scheduled.
Fall Semester	Participate in career center programs when offered. Subjects could include how to write a resume and cover letter, interviewing techniques, aptitude tests, and so on.
	Make decisions on what type of work you want to do and where, geographically, you would like to do it.
November	Write preliminary resume and cover letter. Have them reviewed by a competent adult.
December	Finalize your resume and cover letter. Remember, adjustments to these documents are permitted at any time.

So you see, there's lots to be accomplished. The danger is that, with all there is to do, you will skimp in the preparation phase—do less than is necessary. Complete preparation is the best chance you have of succeeding in securing great job interviews. Let's begin this stage with a discussion of your geographic and job preferences.

10. Geographic and Job Preferences

Before you begin to market yourself, you must answer two very important questions. The first is perhaps the most important decision you will make: What do I want to do? What type of work am I interested in? What kind of position do I want?

In this book, there will be no in-depth effort made to help you select your career preferences. This is a highly individual challenge that only you can address. But the importance of making that determination early cannot be overstated.

> *Knowing where you are going greatly*
> *improves your chances of getting there.*

Most importantly, do not begin marketing yourself until you know where you're going. The direction you select is a very important consideration, as you will find out. However, in focusing on your career preferences, let's see if we can help you along a little.

While very few freshmen have any idea what they ultimately might like to do, the evaluation of career alternatives should be substantially under way by your senior year. In effect, you have had four years to decide on a specific career, and the senior year is the time to finalize those plans.

What to Do

"How do students decide on a career direction?" you ask. There are several ways. First, many take extensive aptitude tests while in college. These tests are designed to assist you in learning more about your own aptitudes. The tests will guide you in what you are, and are not, capable of doing. Many include identifying types of work you are capable of performing. Some go further and identify specific industries in which you could excel and specific job functions within those industries. Armed with this information, you can go forward with the comfort of knowing which careers to pursue and which ones to avoid.

Aids to Answering the Age-Old Question: "What Do I Want to Do?"

✔ Aptitude Tests*	✔ Internships
✔ Summer Employment	✔ Career Books*
✔ Daily Observations	✔ Parents
✔ Successful Businesspeople	✔ Guidance Counselors*

See Chapter 11, "Career Centers."

During the undergraduate years, students have a number of opportunities to observe and be exposed to many job possibilities. This exposure comes through ordinary daily activities. Students need to be alert to what they are seeing and hearing day to day in the context of career opportunities. The problem is that students often don't take advantage of opportunities presented to them. They are simply not alert enough to learn from their daily experiences, and thus lose many chances to focus on career choices.

Another valuable tool in determining future career paths is through summer employment. Of course, students who don't have work experience will not be able to learn about various business opportunities. Additionally, you will have learned little about future business possibilities if you have had miscellaneous summer jobs (those receiving one rating point on the Experience Rater).

Students, however, who have business-related work experience, apart from its value on the resume, stand to benefit significantly when evaluating future career choices. Remember, positions that earn a three- or five-point credit on the Experience Rater are usually 9-to-5-type jobs in normal business environments. These experiences can be enormously helpful in providing employment guidance for the future. In many cases, the result is not finding out what you would like to do but, instead, learning what you don't want to do. Both are equally valuable results of summer work.

Internships provide valuable insight into future career paths. An internship is usually a summer business job (though there are some that are year-round) that is often looked upon by employers as a testing ground for next year's college graduates. It is also an opportunity for the intern to evaluate whether the work being performed is a suitable business possibility for the future. Internships are a great learning experience as well as an opportunity to sufficiently impress the employer to produce a job offer for you upon graduation.

Let's examine another source that could assist you in determining your best career direction—people around you whose opinion you value. These are people who, on the one hand, know you pretty well and, on the other hand, are familiar with the business world. Usually, these people have significant business experience.

Parental Advice

Start with your parents. It's not true that your parents' advice ranks just below that of your worst enemy. In fact, it's probably the best counseling you'll get if you can overcome the natural reluctance to ask for it. Parents know you best, perhaps even better than you do, and while they may or may not be comfortably conversant about the business world, they will have keen insight into what your talents are and the areas in which you fall short. Additionally, in many cases, parents have business experience, and it should be rewarding to put the two together. This counseling process with your parents need not be at a formal sit-down meeting. It can be held less formally over time. A simple, sincerely stated question like the following could start the ball rolling, "Dad, what businesses do you think I should go into?" Rest assured, Dad will be flattered you asked and will usually make valuable contributions.

In addition to your parents as career direction guidance counselors, you should seek out assistance from others you respect. These are often people you know who are experienced in the business world. As I have mentioned earlier, many young people have approached me for advice, not because I'm a professional guidance counselor, but because they have learned from others that I can relate to their needs and that I have valuable advice to give and a willingness to give it. There are many people like me available to offer career advice.

These "counselors" can come from your family's circle of friends, from your college professors and administrators, from past summer employers, from leaders of groups in which you are a member, and from relatives. You will be very well rewarded by tapping personal acquaintances for career guidance.

You can see that, with the addition of your college career center, which we will discuss in the next chapter, there is ample help available for you to form your career path. Use all the avenues of help you can and you will have a much better focus on your career preferences.

Where to Do It

The next major question you must answer in the Preparing for the Interview Search stage concerns geography—specifically, in what section of the country do you want to work? The choices can be broad (anywhere in the country) or narrow (in just one specific city).

If you are willing to work anywhere, you can pursue interviews in any city in the country. This flexibility provides you with a very wide assortment of job possibilities. However, this advantage is offset by the cost and time involved in extensive job interviewing in distant locations. Long-distance job searching also reduces your opportunity to meet frequently with prospective employers in person. It is much easier to drop in to a local city office on the spur of the moment for a follow-up appointment than it would be for an out-of-town position. Furthermore, you are more likely to get an interview with a local company if you have a good, but not great, resume than you would with a company located halfway across the country. Lastly, it would be impractical to apply for an out-of-town position utilizing some of the techniques of the Direct Prospecting approach (to be discussed in Chapter 19).

As a result, most college seniors narrow their geographical preferences considerably. The logical alternative to pursuing positions anywhere in the country is to focus on one specific city. Then the main consideration is whether your college is located in the city where you want to work, or whether you are interested in a different city. The simplest choice, of course, is to pursue employment in the same city as your school—primarily because it is easier to interview for positions that might be open and because the university often generates goodwill in the local job market.

If you are determined to seek a position in or near your hometown, keep in mind that you will face many of the same expenses and time burdens as in any long-distance job search. It has been my experience that, because of the difficulties of seeking interviews from long range, students who plan to work in their hometown tend to do much of their interviewing after they have graduated, not before.

When to Do It

This brings up an important point: I strongly urge you to set a goal to obtain your job *before* graduation, not after. If you wait until after graduation, employers will wonder what problems you have had that have prevented you from getting a job before graduation, or they will express concern about your level of ambition and effort. Finally, many job openings are filled during the spring semester, and by summer there are fewer available openings.

Needless to say, the individual seeking employment in one specific location will uncover fewer job opportunities. Depending on the type of work you are seeking, you may be faced with very limited choices in one location and find it necessary to expand your employment horizon.

I know of one college senior who marketed himself extremely well in one city, but to no avail. He found a depressed economy in his target city. It was a localized condition that required him to broaden his geographical view. Ultimately, he was successful in his job search but in a city a thousand miles away.

To effectively market your talents, you must know where to aim your rifle before you pull the trigger.

You can see from this brief discussion how important it is to determine what you want to do and where you want to do it before you begin your personal marketing program. If you do not properly address these two issues, your interview search can flounder and become directionless.

11. Career Centers

In the interview search process, the biggest asset you have at your disposal is your university's career center. Each school may give its department a different name and vary its duties, but in all cases, career centers are loaded with a rich array of information, advice, and counseling.

Career centers are active departments geared to helping you obtain employment upon graduation. A primary career center function is arranging interviews between college seniors and corporations in the market for educated, entry-level people. Because this is such a significant activity of career centers, we will devote an entire chapter to it in the following section—Marketing Yourself. However, a career center can do much more for you, so read on.

Frankly, I'm a big fan of career centers. In many schools and with many students, the career center is an underused asset, and that defies logic. On the one hand, we have a bunch of students who know very little about business careers and even less on how to pursue them. On the other hand, we have a professionally staffed department that exists solely to answer students' questions and provide employment counseling and guidance. Despite the fact that career centers work very hard to help those most willing to use their services, many students use career centers superficially at best. Very few young people I have worked with (including my own children) have made much use of their school's career center. In discussions I have had with career center directors, I am constantly amazed at the breadth of services career centers offer and how little use is made of them. If you get nothing else from this book, at least walk away from it determined to walk into your career center and put your future in their hands. It will pay off handsomely.

> *Participating in your career center's activities before interviews will increase your interviewing successes.*

Let's take a little time here to review what a career center can do for you and how you can benefit from its assistance. The goal of most career centers is to assist students in preparing for their job search. Looking at it as a complete package, the career center stays with the student throughout the employment search process. They do that by providing help at each stage of the student's job search. Here's how they do it.

Checking Your Aptitude

Most career centers provide programs to help you focus on your potential work preference through the use of aptitude tests. One school I know of offers the Campbell Interest and Skill Survey complete with data collection, a short test, and a concluding evaluation of the results. In addition, this school offers SIGIPLUS, a computer service that connects your skills, interests, and values with possible occupations and then provides you with in-depth information about these occupations. Another assessment tool is the SDS (Self-Directed Search), which helps you discover your vocational personality and connects this to work environments where you could be happiest and most productive. Other schools offer different programs, but they are all designed to help you assess your capabilities and provide direction on where these assets can be best utilized.

Virtually all career centers provide some form of guidance counseling. As always, every school does it differently but all give you an opportunity to meet with an employment specialist, who is 100 percent on your side. These meetings can take many directions, including vocational assessment, practical employment search information, and descriptions of many occupations, to name a few, and most importantly, a friendly ear anxious to help. Remember these are professionally trained people who know much more about job searching than you do. Use them!

Most career centers have a library of reference and self-help material including books, pamphlets, articles—all to provide you with additional assistance in your search. These libraries include information on career choices, job descriptions, potential employers, resume writing, interviewing, knowledge of companies, cover letters, and much, much more. It is another great aspect of your university's career center.

As you will learn, the importance of your resume cannot be overstated. It is the key document in your arsenal. Help in creating a good resume, apart from this book, can be obtained from career center libraries, as well as directly from career center counselors. The counselor, for example, can assist you in preparing your resume or by simply reviewing your completed one for accuracy, grammar, and punch. All resumes, and for that matter all cover letters, need careful review. The career center can do that for you.

Interview Preparation

Perhaps the biggest advantage offered to you by your career center is its interviewing preparation program. In many cases, it provides pointers on how to conduct yourself in an interview, offers a list of commonly asked questions by corporations, and makes reading material available on the interview process, to name a few. Many schools will arrange mock interviews for you in which a career counselor will role-play the employer and you, of course, will role-play the job applicant. Some schools videotape mock interviews, providing a terrific opportunity for you and the counselor to critique the interview and develop interviewing strategies. Videotaping mock interviews can be more valuable than almost any other service provided by career centers (except actual job interviews). No one should enter into a real interview without having role-played in mock interviews.

Because most job interviews are held the same time each year, career centers find it effective to conduct workshops on employment searches. In fact, many schools require students who plan to participate in on-campus interviewing to attend a job search orientation program before they are allowed to utilize the interviewing services of the career center. This orientation workshop generally includes a broad review of strategies for finding a job along with an explanation of the procedures for on-campus interviewing.

Career Center Workshop Programs
1. **Resume Preparation**
2. **Writing the Cover Letter**
3. **Career Goals**
4. **Developing a Job Search Strategy**
5. **Interviewing Techniques**
6. **Making Contacts**
7. **Identifying Your Special Skills**
8. **Targeting Jobs**

This has been a brief overview of what a good career center can do for you. Make no mistake, getting a good job is tough work. A million and a half students each year flood the employment market looking for the best jobs, and many of them are extremely well prepared. You must be also. Job seeking is no different from any other competition. The best trained, the most talented, and the most aggressive will win. Your career center will give you an advantage, but only if you will use it.

If I really wanted to maximize my job search efforts, I'd venture into my career center well before the spring interviewing session and begin to learn what it offers me in the way of career planning. You will be that much further ahead of your competition when it comes time to "play ball."

12. The Resume

Most employers decide who to interview based solely on one or a combination of the following—the cover letter, the resume, and the approach used by the applicant. In this chapter, you will read about the importance of having a superior resume. Following that, you will learn how to write an outstanding resume. Later, you will be led through a well-crafted cover letter and finally, in the Marketing Yourself section, you will be shown approaches to use on targeted companies. Of these, the resume is the most important.

Before we begin our discussion of the resume, let's take a look at what happens when you send a resume and cover letter to a prospective employer. Perhaps knowledge of my personal review process would be helpful.

In the course of any month, I receive fifteen to twenty unsolicited resumes—twelve months a year. This occurs even though I may have no positions open. When I am actively seeking job candidates, the number of resumes received swells geometrically. These resumes come by mail, by fax, and by personal delivery. Most, but interestingly enough not all, are accompanied by a cover letter. Follow-up phone calls from applicants occur in only about 5 percent of the resumes (more on this later).

What happens when I receive a resume? If I have no position available, I scan the cover letter then review the resume for about fifteen *seconds!* Each application gets a same-day thank you/rejection letter. My response letter is sent promptly so that I can avoid follow-up calls from applicants.

When I am looking for an individual to fill a position, I will double my resume review time to thirty *seconds*. In reviewing candidates, I know what I am looking for, and thirty seconds is about all the time I need to spot relevant characteristics. Those resumes that don't meet my needs receive a prompt response; those who have initially interesting traits are put aside for more careful examination.

You can see from this description that your resume has just a few precious seconds to attract attention. For that reason, the construction of the resume (and cover letter) is very important. So let's get into this vital subject.

The resume is a personal document that summarizes your various experiences—most of which were achieved during your college days. As you might suspect, when the second semester of your senior year rolls around, your resume ingredients are nearly fixed. In other words, those items that make your resume stand out are those you created as you went along—not added hastily in the twilight of your senior year.

The Selling Document

At any point in a person's career, the resume is the most significant document a job applicant can produce. When given or sent to a company, its primary goal is to catch someone's attention and be strong enough to generate an interview. Therefore, the resume must include a compendium of relevant experiences presented in a positive, concise manner. From it, most job interviews are granted or rejected. In the next chapters, we will discuss actually writing the resume and constructing the cover letter that usually accompanies the resume. You will learn further that the employer considers the cover letter to be an inferior product to the resume. The resume is composed of facts (not necessarily all the facts, as you will see shortly); the accompanying letter serves to introduce the resume. Professional interviewers will make their decision to interview a potential candidate based primarily on the resume, that is, on the applicant's credentials.

> *The resume is a selling document,*
> *not an autobiography.*

Make no mistake, the resume is a written sales pitch. Virtually all resumes that fail to produce interviews fail because they do not sell sufficiently well enough or because the individual's background simply doesn't fit the position being sought. Since the idea that the resume is a selling document may be new to you, let's discuss this thought.

As we suggested earlier, put yourself in the position of an interviewer. Over a period of time, the interviewer will see many resumes. Most will be well prepared, look good, and provide information about the applicant. How does the interviewer make the decision on which applicant to interview? The answer is both easy and complicated. The easy part is that the decision will be based on the relative merits (at least in the eyes of the interviewer) of each resume. The complicated part is that each interviewer (and each available job) is different, and thus each will respond differently to the various ingredients of the resumes.

Only Positives Allowed

Now, perhaps we can all agree on the following: a resume containing positive ingredients, stated positively, has a better chance of producing an interview than a resume with positive ingredients stated negatively or, worse yet, negative ingredients described in any manner. My guess is that you would agree with this premise. If you think about it, you will find that this approach is exactly what salespeople use. Whatever it is that salespeople sell, they make every effort to stress the positives, and they do so by talking positively about them. That's selling, pure and simple.

A job applicant must do the same. With the resume, you are taking perhaps your first step into the world of selling. The resume is not an oral sales pitch, but it is indeed a written one. More importantly, it is the principal, and only, sales message the interviewer will usually receive before granting an interview, and it is upon that document that the decision to interview or not is normally made.

I hope the message is clear. With the exception of a few required salient facts, a good resume should consist of positive points stated positively. Any item on the resume (aside from basic data) that is not a positive in some form *should be minimized or not included.* And, if there is a positive which for some reason cannot be presented positively, it should be downplayed as well.

Some of you will have reservations about eliminating part of your background from the resume—those items that may not enhance the application. You will be quick to argue that a resume is intended to provide an overall picture of a candidate so that the employer can make some value judgments concerning the applicant's possibilities.

At the risk of offending, let me state categorically that that position is wrong. You are under no legal or moral obligation to point out your weaknesses in a resume, nor is there any requirement to provide all the facts about your life and/or your qualifications. In seeking a job interview, your goal is to sell employers on interviewing you, not to give them reasons to reject you. The pursuit of basic information about you is the responsibility of the interviewer. She performs the function of obtaining in-depth knowledge of the applicant's assets and liabilities primarily in two ways—through the personal interview and from the company application form. It is on the application form that you are required to provide the company with the information they request—whether it serves your purposes or not. In fact, any misstatement of fact on an application, whether by design or accident, is grounds for dismissal from many companies today.

Resume Info

Before we move on to the resume itself, let's restate the three premises we have just introduced:

1. The resume is a sales document.
2. The resume should include positive points stated positively.
3. The resume should leave the pursuit of negatives to the interviewer.

With those thoughts in mind, let's talk about the resume in general. First, each resume should contain the following basic data:

1. Name
2. Home address and phone
3. School address and phone

While most of this information is of little value in getting an interview, its importance is obvious.

Everything else on your resume should be positive points stated positively. Remember, the resume is a selling document. Because getting a job interview is a selling job, let's take for a moment a very short course in selling. For example, buying a light bulb: How do you decide which light bulb you will buy if four brands are displayed side by side in a store? Chances are you will select a particular light bulb because it costs less, or lasts longer, or shines brighter, and so on. In other words, you buy one light bulb over another because you perceive that one is in some way better than the others. Chances are you won't buy one bulb over another strictly on the claim that it is a good light bulb. Manufacturers have to differentiate their light bulb from the competition and they can do so by featuring a lower price, or a longer-life bulb, or a brighter bulb, and so on. In other words, they sell you the bulb by pointing out that the bulb is better (in some way) than the competition. As they say in sales, "Sell the sizzle, not the steak."

So it is with you and your resume. The fact that you have graduated from college is not enough to differentiate you from thousands of other college students who have done the same. You must sell yourself by pointing out that your college experiences make you a better candidate than your competition.

Where Do You Excel?

Delve further into your experiences and ask yourself what makes you better than the competition. Grades, for example? Perhaps. If you had a 3.5 grade point average (out of a possible 4.0), that makes you a better candidate (at least based on grades) than the applicant with a 2.9 grade point average, but a poorer candidate than someone with a 3.9 grade point average. At the risk of generalizing, anyone with a grade point average below 3.0 should not include it on the resume. There will be many applicants with higher marks. If you are applying for a position that usually requires very bright candidates, you should leave off your grade point average if it's below 3.5.

You may now be thinking that interviewers will ultimately learn of your grade point average anyway, so why shouldn't you simply tell them initially? Several reasons, actually. First, they may not care about grades as much as you think—but you don't know that when you send in your resume. Why risk not getting an interview because of a 2.9 GPA? Second, it is the interviewers' responsibility to learn all the salient facts—let them earn their pay. They may not even ask about your GPA. Third, there may be an intriguing reason why your grades are average, and the interview will be the time to explain that. If you are rejected for the interview because of your grade point average, you will not have the opportunity, for example, to explain that your average grades were the result of your need to work full time or your broad participation in extracurricular activities or your need to help at home. Finally, the interview gives you the chance to sell yourself, regardless of grades, but you lose that opportunity if you don't get the interview.

The same reasoning applies throughout the resume. You must emphasize the good parts of your background while avoiding those that are not. By now, you can see how important it is for college students to have resume selling points from their four years at school. Without them, your resume could effectively be blank.

As an interviewer, my most important task is to discover which of the many applicants I have would be the most successful in performing the duties of an available job. Therefore, your resume must project to me your potential for future success. How do you do that? You do that by showing me that you already have successes to your credit. It is a truism that a person who is generally successful will usually always be successful. Why does it seem that a high school leader becomes a college leader? Why does a standout in college become a business standout? Why do students selected "most likely to succeed" usually succeed? It doesn't matter what you do as long as you succeed at it. Successful students get more and better job interviews.

Peer Successes

As an employer, how do I measure success in a student? Perhaps the best measurement is the achievement level you attained versus your peer group. For example, if you are elected to important positions by your peers, you have succeeded. That's the kind of candidate the employer wants to interview. Consequently, your resume should focus on peer-level successes.

Examples of Peer-Level Successes

1. **If you graduate from a very top university in your given field as opposed to the many other colleges throughout the country, you already have a measure of success because you were accepted at and graduated from a higher-rated school than most in your peer group.**
2. **If your major matches your job preference, you are ahead of much of your competition because many of them do not have good major/career matches.**
3. **If your marks are high, you have outperformed the bulk of your competition.**
4. **If you were involved in campus activities and had leadership positions in some (or all) of them, you have outperformed your peers.**
5. **If you have had successful, pertinent business experience along the way, you will excel when compared to your competition.**
6. **If you have had one (or more) unique life experiences, you will stand out in a crowd of applicants.**

To have a success-oriented resume, you should have begun your preparation early and focused on being successful in the six major resume ingredients. If you have successes (once again, defined as achieving above your peer group) in all six categories, you will have your pick of most any job interview. If you were successful in some of these areas, you will still get good interviews. But if you had limited success in all six categories, you will obtain less attractive job interviews.

Whither the Job Objective?

One of the most often-asked questions about the resume is whether it should contain a job objective statement. The answer is no! Although there might be a few exceptions to this rule, the job objective should be included instead in the cover letter, not the resume, for several very important reasons.

The first and main reason for omitting the job objective from the resume goes back to the resume's purpose. It is a selling document. Stating a job objective in the resume is not a selling point. In fact, it could be a deterrent. Including a job objective in the resume dilutes the sales effort of the resume.

The second reason is probably the most obvious. If your job objective is to become an accountant at a CPA firm and you state that in your resume, what happens if you either fail to get an accounting job or decide after interviewing for one that you no longer want that type of work? Your resume needs to be redone. If you state your job objective in the cover letter, (since each one is typed individually), it is easy enough to change your objective without redoing the resume.

A third reason for not including your job objective in the resume is to avoid confusion if you are seeking more than one type of job. This is more prevalent among college students than people already in the work force, because many students don't know exactly what they want to do. If the job objective is included in the resume, you will need three different resumes if you are pursuing three different types of jobs. I can see it now—sooner or later, you're going to put the resume with the marketing job objective in the envelope going to the accounting firm.

Finally, students generally have little understanding of specific jobs that are available in business. They know some job titles, such as accountant, engineer, salesperson, and so on, but most companies have several levels for each type of position and most have specific job descriptions. It is unlikely that an inexperienced student could write a job objective that matches a specific available job. The interviewer will know very early that the applicant has limited knowledge of a specific job. In fact, in some cases the student may have no knowledge of what job, if any, a prospective company might have open. In these situations, students often resort to generalized job objectives, and these are best included in the cover letter.

Whither Personal References?

Another question that comes up frequently when discussing the resume is whether personal references should be included. With few exceptions, references rarely enhance the resume.

Most interviewers know that the references you provide are people who will have positive things to say about you. As a result, the information gained from a reference check is not likely to be enlightening or unbiased. Good interviewers occasionally mine some interesting items as they check your references, but usually they just get favorable input.

There are two exceptions to the rule of excluding references from the resume: an individual who is well known in the industry in which you are pursuing a position would add sizzle to your resume, and someone who is a well-known person overall would also spice up the resume. However, most students are not fortunate enough to have high-powered, notable references; thus resume references usually add little to the sales pitch.

Finally, exclude references from the resume because reference checking is usually done during the interviewing process, not before the first interview. With the two exceptions mentioned above, the place to provide references is on the company job application, not the resume.

Action Words!

What about the use of action words in the resume? An action word is a descriptive word about a specific function. Here are a few examples:

1. Directed (a radio station program)
2. Organized (a new student committee)
3. Illustrated (a college publication)
4. Upgraded (a fraternity project)
5. Facilitated (the introduction of a new project)
6. Instrumental (in achieving an end result)

Handle action words with care. While it may seem like a small thing, there are two types of action words. The first one describes the activity cited and is factual; the second judges the success of the undertaking and is subjective. From the list above, *directed, organized,* and *illustrated* are descriptive; *upgraded, facilitated,* and *instrumental* are quality judgments of success.

As an employer, I prefer descriptive action words and greatly dislike evaluatory action words. Students rarely have the experience to make accurate judgments on the quality of their efforts, and employers know it. A qualitative action word does not usually impress the potential employer because it sounds like bragging and it may not be an accurate reflection of the success of the task. Remember, in using action words, descriptions of functions count more than the student's judgment of his or her success.

Many resumes I receive include a section entitled "Interests and Hobbies" or something like that. The fact that an applicant enjoys tennis or stamp collecting is generally useless information. Unless the applicant has an outside interest that relates directly to the position being sought, it is of no value on the resume. Remember, the resume should only include positive ingredients (for the job) stated positively.

In summary, the resume should include six types of information:

1. Basic data—name, address, school attended, and so on
2. Major(s) taken—related, it is hoped, to the job being sought
3. Grade point averages—if they are positive
4. Activities with leadership roles
5. Related significant work experiences
6. Unique life experiences and other successes

Once you have amassed all the information noted above, it is important that you create your own resume. You must organize it, select the appropriate ingredients, write it out, and review it yourself. Recently, after a two-hour meeting with one young man, he sent me a follow-up letter with a question: "Would you be so good as to help me formulate a resume and cover letter to send to firms?" My response to his request was no, I would not help him formulate his resume and letter, but I would critique it after he had completed its preparation. All initial job seekers need to sweat out the construction of the resume and letter to enable them to build on that experience for future resumes.

At the risk of stating the obvious, resumes and cover letters that appear attractive will likely receive a higher level of attention from interviewers. That means the resume and cover letter should be carefully laid out in a concise and organized fashion. If possible, laser print your resume for best appearance. Choose a font style that is readable and use clean white paper. When you finish your resume and cover letter, give them to a disinterested associate to review both for content and appearance.

It might be of value to summarize some of the important No-Nos of resume preparation.

Resume Top Ten No-Nos
1. **Including job objectives**
2. **Including personal references**
3. **Using qualitative action words**
4. **Resumes longer than one page**
5. **Resumes containing grammatical errors**
6. **Producing an unattractive resume**
7. **References to religion or national origin**
8. **Reference to salary requirements**
9. **Including a personal photograph**
10. **"Interests & Hobbies" section**

Later in this book are a number of actual college student resumes. Each is critiqued, with good and bad features noted, to help you recognize many of the points made in this section. After you read the next chapter, "Writing the Resume," review these sample resumes. It will make writing your resume much easier.

Remember the resume is a selling document, not an autobiography. Now, let's look at how to write the resume. The next chapter will help you create an outstanding one.

13. Writing the Resume

As we have said on numerous occasions, the resume is your primary job search document, the one that sells you best. From it, employers will determine whether you get an interview or not—thus a lot rides on it.

Preparing the resume is a major task. Therefore, to approach this in an organized fashion, we're going to create a mythical student—Robert G. Wilson—whose goal is to work for an accounting firm upon graduation. Wilson, as you will see, is an outstanding young man. His mythical resume emphasizes the importance of leading with your strengths, to include only salient points, and to develop the resume as a selling document.

While Wilson's resume will be an excellent one, you can vary the format to match your own situation. You must make sure the resume is clean, neat, and efficient—just what the interviewer wants to see. With so many resumes to plow through, employers will view the easy-to-read ones in a positive way. In constructing the resume, put yourself in the place of the reader. What would you like to see in a resume if you were the employer? Among other things, of course, you would want to see it free of grammatical and typographical errors and without hype. And you would also want it to be readable and informative.

There are five major sections of a college graduate's first resume:

1. Name and Address(es)
2. Education and Academics
3. Activities
4. Employment
5. Additional Successes

Let's start with the name and address section—simple enough. In it, you should include your home and college addresses so that the resume can be used after graduation if you do not get a job beforehand. Here's how it can look:

ROBERT G. WILSON

<u>School</u>
147 Arkansas Street
Albuquerque, NM 87110
505/654-8122

<u>Home</u>
7412 Cherry Lane
Spring Lake, NJ 07762
609/821-8745

It is extremely important that someone is at each phone to answer incoming calls in a professional manner. Employers are rarely willing to call more than once or twice before moving on to the next applicant. At the least, use of a telephone answering device is mandatory, and the message it gives should be brief, to the point, and devoid of humor.

As you can see, there is nothing complex about the address section.

Let's turn our attention now to the second part of the resume—education and academics. This portion should include all elements of your academic experience: the name of your school, your graduation date, degree(s), major (and minors), grade point average (if appropriate), academic awards, honors, and talents. Let's see how Bob Wilson's academic history looks on his resume:

EDUCATION AND ACADEMICS:

Decatur College, May 1996
Degree—B.S. in Accounting
Major—Accounting; Minor—English
Grade Point Average—3.8 in major; 3.6 in all subjects
Academic Awards—Robert Jones Scholarship—4 years
—Accounting Award of Merit
Academic Talents—Computer Literate

Wilson's academic achievements are quite impressive, and they are enhanced by their presentation on the resume. Concise, with no extraneous material. The only items in this section that aren't entirely clear are the type of scholarship Wilson received and what the Accounting Award of Merit was. These can be elaborated on in the resume if they enhance it; if not, they can be left as is.

Note the use of two grade point averages. Because they are excellent, they can both be used. You are free to use any grade point average you choose—GPA in your major or in all your subjects—whichever is better. You can even use the grade point average for your last two years if it is your best GPA. It will send a message to the interviewer that you really went to work in your junior and senior years and improved your academic performance significantly. Use the GPA that paints you in the best light. If your grades are under a 3.0, your best strategy is to omit any mention of them.

You will also note that Wilson's resume does not include a list of courses taken in college. Courses offered in a major seldom vary much from one school to another, so there is little to be gained by listing them. Furthermore, most available jobs are not based on specific courses you might have taken. Employers are more interested in how well you did in your courses.

Also absent from the resume is a description of the specific computer experience Wilson has. Most employers want to know if an applicant is computer experienced. If you're adept at some programs, employers reason, you can learn their company's computer requirements. An exception to this rule is if the student is pursuing a technical computer-oriented job. Then a listing of your specific computer expertise would be appropriate.

The next section presents Wilson's nonacademic achievements (in essence what he did when he wasn't studying). It is not necessary to include all of your activities on the resume if some of them don't contribute to your success picture. As you will see, Wilson was very active. It is interesting to note that he achieved above the level of his peers in all four listed activities. Remember, employers are seeking success-oriented people. Wilson has a varied and full activity record and a successful one as well. Here it is:

ACTIVITIES: Accounting Society—three years; Chairman in senior year
Phi Delta Phi Fraternity—Social Chairman, Rush Chairman
   Winner—The Phi Award—Dedication
Football—Varsity, three years
   All-Conference Wide Receiver
Kite and Key College Greeters—two years; Chairman in
   senior year

Once again, the presentation is neat and concise. It shows several activities, all different, denoting wide interests, and all completed with success. He was chairman of two organizations, a stellar athlete, and an award winner in his fraternity life. Notice Wilson decided to explain what the Phi Award was because he believes it improves his resume. It does.

The next section summarizes Wilson's employment history. In his case, he only worked summers because his academics and activities left him little time to work while at school. This in no way reduces the strength of Wilson's background. An applicant does not need to work all the time, but he should show employment during the summers. Of course, if you had no school activities, average marks, and no work history during the school year, employers would wonder about the amount of time you wasted at school. Here is Wilson's work history:

EMPLOYMENT: Summer 1992—Camp Towanda—Counselor
Summer 1993—Cafe Chocolate—Waiter
Summer 1994—Public Service Gas Co. —Accounts Receivable Dept. Processed monthly customer bills, received payments, pursued delinquencies, handled customer inquiries.
Summer 1995—Theodore Martin CPA
Assisted small CPA practice, working alternately in the commercial and individual departments. Worked with tax returns, monthly payrolls, and financial projections. Assisted partner in client contacts.

You will note at least three things of interest in this section of the resume. First, there is no mention of work experience before college. That work is usually labor intensive and of no particular value in an interview search. Second, there is no explanation of the duties of the camp counselor and waiter positions. These are universal functions readily understood by most everyone. Furthermore, they do not significantly enhance the resume so there is no need for elaboration.

Third, employment experience is listed chronologically starting with the first job. Many experts argue that the most recent position should be mentioned first so that the one most likely to be of value in the resume is seen first. Others suggest the best job, resumewise, should be cited first. While there is validity to both points of view, I personally prefer to see the progression of positions from least significant to most important so that I can size up an applicant's forward momentum. And I like them in chronological order as well.

The job descriptions shown for Wilson's positions with Public Service Gas Co. and Theodore Martin CPA are extremely valuable, and they read excellently. Firms seeking an accounting employee will look at this experience with great enthusiasm. In both jobs he had varied activities, mostly related to accounting work in one way or another, and he had client contact activity at both firms—valuable experience for most any job today.

The final element of Wilson's work experience is its consistency—he worked every summer—gradually progressing in levels of responsibility, content, and importance. Just what the interviewer is looking for.

The last section of the resume may be the most powerful of them all. As I have mentioned, successful people usually get the best jobs. Thus it is important to give the employer all the "success ammunition" you have. I have titled this major segment of the resume "Additional Successes." You will rarely see it mentioned in books on resume writing.

Most resumes document your college accomplishments. But some of your successes may not fit the resume format and could therefore be lost from it. Why not a special section for your successes?

Bob Wilson's resume is loaded with accomplishments. However, Wilson (and you?) have other successes not shown elsewhere on the resume. As a result, the employer may never know about them. So, following the employment category, include an Additional Successes section that allows you to enumerate lifetime accomplishments not shown elsewhere on the resume. Those unique life experiences not already cited in your resume can be included in this section. Take a look at Wilson's additional successes:

ADDITIONAL
SUCCESSES: 1991—Lead role in high school play, "The Crucible"
1996—Nominee for the College's four top Senior Class Awards

This section focuses the interviewer's attention on successes not described previously. When the employer finishes reviewing your resume, you want him to say to himself, "This guy looks good, let's get him in here for an interview." He's more likely to say that if he sees a lot of successes.

How Does Wilson Rate?

How does Wilson check out on the Experience Rater? Pretty well, as you might suspect. Wilson receives five points for the Course of Study category since his major and degree (accounting) are in the same field as the position he is seeking. He receives an additional five points in the Academic Achievement section because his grade point average is over 3.5, and he receives another point for earning an academic award—the Accounting Award of Merit. He also earns five points for his extracurricular activities because he had several activities. He was a leader in some of them and a success in all of them. Give him an extra point for winning the Phi Award and being named All-Conference Wide Receiver.

Wilson also garners five points for his outside employment because for two years it was directly related to the work he was seeking. Wilson has no unique life experience so he would receive no points for that. Because additional successes are difficult to measure from one student to another, we give no point credit for them. However, as in the case of Wilson's additional successes, they certainly enhance the resume. The only section of the resume we can't rate in Wilson's Experience Rater is the college he attended. We have used a fictitious school name so we can make no point judgment. Nonetheless, Wilson's resume is outstanding, he should get an excellent position in his field, and that task should be accomplished over a reasonable period of time.

You will notice several omissions from Wilson's resume. There is no job objective included, which, as you have learned, rightfully belongs in the cover letter. Factual information on Wilson, such as age, marital status, and so on, is also excluded. As a current college graduate, that information is obvious and/or immaterial. The perennial subject of "interests and hobbies" is not present in Wilson's resume because in his case they didn't lend any credibility to the job search. Most hobbies and interests are unrelated to employment. Finally, as we pointed out in Chapter 12, "The Resume," personal references were excluded because they did not include notable people. They should, however, be available later on in the interviewing process at the request of the company.

Now that we have constructed Wilson's resume, let's take a look at it in its entirety. It really does the job and advances Wilson's credentials significantly.

ROBERT G. WILSON

School
147 Arkansas Street
Albuquerque, NM 87110
505/654-8122

Home
7412 Cherry Lane
Spring Lake, NJ 07762
609/821-8745

EDUCATION AND ACADEMICS:
Decatur College, May 1996
Degree—B.S. in Accounting
Major—Accounting; Minor—English
Grade Point Average—3.8 in major; 3.6 in all subjects
Academic Awards—Robert Jones Scholarship—4 years
—Accounting Award of Merit
Academic Talents—Computer Literate

ACTIVITIES:
Accounting Society—three years; Chairman in senior year
Phi Delta Phi Fraternity—Social Chairman, Rush Chairman
Winner—The Phi Award—Dedication
Football—Varsity, three years
All-Conference Wide Receiver
Kite and Key College Greeters—two years; Chairman in senior year

EMPLOYMENT:	Summer 1992—Camp Towanda—Counselor
	Summer 1993—Cafe Chocolate—Waiter
	Summer 1994—Public Service Gas Co. —Accounts Receivable Dept. Processed monthly customer bills, received payments, pursued delinquencies, handled customer inquiries.
	Summer 1995—Theodore Martin CPA Assisted small CPA practice, working alternately in the commercial and individual departments. Worked with tax returns, monthly payrolls, and financial projections. Assisted partner in client contacts.

ADDITIONAL	
SUCCESSES:	1991—Lead role in high school play, "The Crucible"
	1996—Nominee for the College's four top Senior Class Awards

Resumes Critiqued

Following this section are five actual resumes I have received—with names and addresses excluded. Each is critiqued for content and rated on the Experience Rater scale. As you review these resumes, look for the bracketed numbers and the corresponding underlined portions of each resume. Then match these numbers with the explanation in the "CRITIQUING THE RESUME" section that follows each resume. From this you will note what can be powerful resume ingredients and what shouldn't be included in a resume. One weakness on many resumes is the failure to adequately describe resume activities that stand out, such as awards and honors. Naming an award without describing it reduces its effectiveness considerably.

The evaluation for Resume Six is blank. This is an opportunity for you to test your knowledge about resumes. You may rate that resume using the Experience Rater. Compare your evaluation with mine, which follows Resume Six.

Remember the resume is a selling document, not an autobiography. Eliminate items that do not add to your luster; include those that do. Please have some knowledgeable person review your resume before it is published—you may avoid many pitfalls.

RESUME ONE

Present Address   **Permanent Address**

[1] OBJECTIVE   Seeking an entry level position with an industrial
organization or a financial corporation as a
management or sales trainee and earning
advancement to an officer position.

EDUCATION   **The University of Texas at Arlington**,
Arlington, Texas
B.B.A. major in Finance, May 1996.
[2]   Overall GPA: 3.00.
[3]   Relevant courses include Multinational
Finance, Management of Financial Institutions,
Intermediate Accounting, Real Estate Practices,
Retailing Principles, and Marketing.

[4] EXPERIENCE   **Peony Restaurant, Fort Worth, Texas**
Summer 1995   *WAITER* - organized and served catered meals   **[5]**
for client meetings and company parties; assisted
the restaurant in customer service duties.

The University of Texas at Arlington
[6]   May 1994 - Dec. 1994   *RESIDENT ASSISTANT* - supervised both
co-ed and male residence halls; administered
housing policies and discipline; initiated and
conducted educational and social programs for
students; provided counseling, referrals, and
leadership opportunities for students in both
residence halls.
Jan. 1994 - May 1994   *OFFICE ASSISTANT* - assisted one of the male
residence halls in the daily business activities.

ORGANIZATIONS &   **Delta Sigma Pi Professional Business**
ACTIVITIES   **Fraternity**
CHAIRMAN, MARKETING/PUBLIC RELA-
TIONS COMMITTEE - coordinated and
designed marketing plans for all chapter events.

Finance Society
MEMBER - affiliated with the National Financial
Management Association, a professional
organization comprised of financial executives,
analysts, professors, and students.

UTA Student Foundation
CHARTER MEMBER - participated in the creation of a public relations organization of student leaders to provide student-alumni networking, fundraising projects; conducted public relations campaigns to attract prospective students to UTA.

International Student Organization
TREASURER - directed and budgeted the organization's accounts; managed a budget of $6,000 for International Week 1994.
COORDINATOR, FUNDRAISING COMMITTEE - generated over $1,000 from a major corporation and other companies for International Week 1994.
PEER ADVISOR - conducted orientation activities to help new international students to adjust to campus life in America.

HONORS & AWARDS Honor Roll
Who's Who Among International Students in American Universities & Colleges
The National Dean's List
Student of the Month, The Great Southwestern Rotary International Club
Participated in the UTA Leadership Conference
Student representative at the UTA Development Board Meeting

SPECIAL SKILLS Fluent in English, Chinese, and Malay language. Computer skills: Lotus 1-2-3, WordPerfect, MicrosoftWord, SuperPaint

INTERESTS Reading, music, camping, canoeing, running, badminton [7]

REFERENCES Available upon request. [7]

CRITIQUING THE RESUME

RESUME ONE

EXPERIENCE RATER

	Points
College Attended	1
Courses of Study	5
Academic Achievement	3
Extracurricular Activities	3
Work Experience	1
Unique Life Experience	0
Total	13

Experience Rating:	Fair

Comment: Difficult to evaluate honors and awards. What honor roll? How can applicant be on National Dean's List with a 3.0 grade point average? What qualifications are necessary to be Rotary Student of the Month? Included in *Who's Who?* This section had the potential to sky-rocket this applicant—but it didn't. Special skills are attractive.

[1] Job objective should be in cover letter.

[2] Grade point average is just barely acceptable for inclusion on resume.

[3] A finance major usually takes these courses. It isn't necessary to enumerate them.

[4] Weak employment experience. Applicant worked only one summer and that was in a low-rated capacity.

[5] There is no need to describe the waiter's job. Everyone knows what a waiter does.

[6] Were resident assistant duties performed over the summer? It looks that way.

[7] Most interests and references are unnecessary on resume.

RESUME TWO

Present Address   **Permanent Address**

QUALIFIED BY   A thorough education in all aspects of finance   [1]
                        combined with an excellent background in eco-
                        nomics and small business computer systems.

EDUCATION
[2] September 1991   College of Business, Southwest Texas State
     to   University, San Marcus, Texas 78666.
     May 1996   BBA Degree May 1996

         Major: Finance. Advanced courses include   [3]
                        Management, Marketing, Computer Information
                        Systems, Small Business Computer Systems,
                        Small Business Management, International
                        Economics, Labor Economics, Money and
                        Banking, Business Finance, Real Estate,
                        Investment Analysis, Legal Environment of
                        Business, Financial Management, Financial
                        Institutions, Case Problems in Finance, and
                        Business Policy

EXPERIENCE
[5] July 1986   Involved in fence building and repair, plumbing
     to   installation and repair; completed sales
     August 1990   transactions over the phone, bookkeeping, and
                       sales of firescreens and fireplace accessories.
                       Bill's Plumbing and Fence Craft, Midland,   [4]
                       Texas. Employed four years working summers,
                       weekends, and holidays.

[6]
[7] May 1992   Servicing and testing of oilfield tubular goods.
     to   Domain Enterprises Inc., Midland, Texas.   [4]
     August 1993   Employed two summers overseeing the
                       hydrostatic testing of oilfield tubular goods.

April 1994 to Present	Experienced in all aspects of bar operations including: security, bar-backing, and cocktail preparation and sales. <u>Green Parrot, Inc., San</u> **[4]** <u>Marcos, Texas</u>.

EXTRACURRICULAR

September 1991 to August 1995	<u>Alpha Tau Omega social fraternity. Offices</u> **[8]** <u>Held: Social Service Chairman, Rush</u> <u>Chairman, Sergeant-at-Arms, Secretary,</u> <u>Judicial Council Member, Treasurer</u>.
November 1995 to February 1996	Participant, AT&T Collegiate Investment Challenge. Finishing 2nd out of 43 SWT participants, 26th out of 562 participants in the State of Texas, and 336th out of 13,974 participants nationwide by achieving a 60.3% gain in total portfolio value within the four-month period.

[9]   REFERENCES   <u>Available upon Request</u>

CRITIQUING THE RESUME

RESUME TWO

EXPERIENCE RATER

	Points
College Attended	1
Courses of Study	2
Academic Achievement	1
Extracurricular Activities	3
Work Experience	3
Unique Life Experience	0
Total	10
Experience Rating:	Fair

Comment: There is nothing here to get excited about. Average school, no indication of academic strength, mundane work experience, limited leadership. Would assume applicant is not success oriented and thus not likely to be a success in the business world.

[1] It's not a bad idea to include this statement.

[2] Applicant took five years to graduate. Why?

[3] It is not necessary to include all of these courses in the resume.

[4] Would have preferred to see the name of companies worked for at the beginning of each position instead of buried in the job description.

[5] It is not advantageous to include high school work experience unless it stands out.

[6] No summer work in 1991. Why?

[7] Several items from this entry:

    1. Was this full-time work or just two summers?

    2. If full-time, it could explain why applicant took five years to graduate.

    3. If so, why did he take a year off from school?

[8] Very active fraternity member but not elected president.

[9] Unnecessary section.

RESUME THREE

Present Address: **Permanent Address:**

[1] **OBJECTIVE:**   A challenging entry level position in the financial
industry.

EDUCATION: Candidate for **Bachelor of Science Degree in
Finance and Economics**
Spring Hill College: Mobile, Alabama; May 1996
[2]   G.P.A. 3.68 / 4.00

**RELEVANT
COURSES:**

Calculus I & II	Business Statistics [3]
Prin. of Economics I & II	Business Law
Prin. of Accounting I & II	Marketing Principles
Intermediate Macroeconomics	Management Principles
Intermediate Microeconomics	Managerial Accounting
Insurance / Risk Management	Financial Management
Money and Financial Markets	Investments
Real Estate Finance	Information Systems
Advanced Financial Management	

**WORK
EXPERIENCE:**   **SPRING HILL COLLEGE:** Mobile, Alabama
Assistant Intramurals Coordinator: responsible for
the men's intramural program; coordinate scheduling
of games and officials. 1995-96 Academic Year.
Resident Assistant: responsible for coordinating
hall activities; directional growth of residents;
operational and atmospheric control of the residence
hall. 1995-96 Academic Year.

MILLER DISTRIBUTING COMPANY:
[4]   Fort <u>worth</u>, Texas
Route Salesman: responsible for marketing,
advertising, sale and delivery of products to
customers' stores. June 1995-Present.
[5]   **Driver's Assistant:** <u>aid</u> driver in completion of sales;
conducted inventory at customers' stores;
[6]   responsible for <u>deliverey</u> of products and construction
of point-of-sale displays. June 1994-95.

CITY OF ARLINGTON: Chester W. Ditto Golf Course: Arlington, Texas
Golf Course Maintenance: responsible for maintaining city golf course; irrigation repair; operation of heavy equipment. May 1992 to June 1994.

Financed 80% of College Education

[7]   HONORS/
      ACTIVITIES: **Sigma Chi Fraternity** (1992-95); **Vice-President** 95-96, responsible for conducting all meetings; **Treasurer** 94-95, responsible for $15,000 budget; Service Projects Chairman 93-94, organized and coordinated all service projects.
      Who's Who Among American College Students
[8]   Senior Advisory Board
      Alpha Sigma Nu Honor Society
      President Interhall Dorm Council (1994-95)
      President Mobile Hall Dorm Council (1994-95)
      Spring Hill Orientation Week Staff; Peer Counselor (1993-1996)
      Academic Dean's List (5 of 7 semesters)
      YMCA Volunteer; Coach soccer, first-second grade
      High School: Varsity athletics; Basketball, 4; Track, 3
[9]   Chaminade Award; Best All-around male student
      National Honor Society

[10] REFERENCES: Available upon request.

CRITIQUING THE RESUME

RESUME THREE

EXPERIENCE RATER

	Points
College Attended	1
Courses of Study	5
Academic Achievement	6
Extracurricular Activities	4
Work Experience	3
Unique Life Experience	0
Total	19

Experience Rating:	Outstanding

Comment: You get the impression this applicant is alive and active. He has a lot of honors and interests. While there is nothing here that would set him far above his peer group, he would still warrant a look.

[1] Put job objective in cover letter.

[2] In addition to a strong grade point average, student has academic honors—Dean's List, National Honor Society—shown further down in the resume. These should have been included in the Education section or in an Additional Successes section.

[3] It is not necessary to list these courses.

[4] "worth" should be "Worth."

[5] "aid" should be "aided."

[6] "deliverey" should be "delivery."

[7] Good activities. Why only occasional bold type? This section should be better organized for reading simplicity and impact.

[8] Since neither Senior Advisory Board nor Alpha Sigma Nu Honor Society are self-descriptive, they should be explained further.

[9] Is the Chaminade Award for high school or college?

[10] Omit reference section.

RESUME FOUR

Campus Address: Home Address:

[1]   CAREER
OBJECTIVE: To obtain a challenging position in retail
financial sales that will allow me to achieve a
high level of success both for my company
and personally.

EDUCATION: CARNEGIE-MELLON UNIVERSITY,
Pittsburgh, PA
[2]   Degree: B.S. Management with a concentration
in *Finance*.
Graduation: May 1996

[3]

BUSINESS
[4]   EXPERIENCE: PROJECT COORDINATOR,
AMERICAN SUNSET, INC.
Acted as a liaison between project manager
and general contractor during the construction
of a high tech office/warehouse building.
Responsibilities included utilizing the critical-
path method and programming the same on the
company's computer system in order to monitor
both cash flow and project timing.
SUMMER 1995, BOCA RATON, FLORIDA

CUSTOMER SERVICE, *SOMFY SYSTEMS, SA.*
Assisted sales representatives in the customer
service department to guarantee total customer
satisfaction with the company's specialized line
of electronics. Somfy controls over 70% of their
market worldwide.
[5]   SUMMER 1994, NICE, FRANCE

ASSISTANT STORE MANAGER,
THE GAP STORES, INC.
Started as a stock clerk and 8 days later was
promoted to assistant manager responsible for
all aspects of operating a retail clothing store,
during which time I consistently broke all of the
store's previous sales records.
SUMMER 1993, NEW YORK, N.Y.

TELEMARKETING REPRESENTATIVE,
HARRIS COMMUNICATIONS
Responsible for cold calling on Controllers of
publicly held companies to market the new
Heidelberg four-color printer as an important
tool for preparing their annual reports.
SUMMER 1992, NEW YORK, N.Y.

TECHNICAL SKILLS: Current user of IBM and Apple Personal
Computers: Able to program in Basic, Pascal,
Lisp, and familiar with many application
packages such as Wordstar, Lotus 1-2-3,
and others.

INTERESTS: Physical fitness, watersports, music, and travel. [6]

PERSONAL: 21 years old, single, self-motivated, and goal [7]
oriented.

[8]   References available upon request

CRITIQUING THE RESUME

RESUME FOUR

EXPERIENCE RATER

	Points
College Attended	3
Courses of Study	3
Academic Achievement	1
Extracurricular Activities	0
Work Experience	5
Unique Life Experience	5
Total	17

Experience Rating:	Very Good

Comment: There is only one area of this resume that stands out—excellent business experience, some related to the position being sought. Otherwise, this is a very ordinary applicant. Employment credentials lift his possibilities significantly. Some extracurricular activities and a 3.0 grade point average would have put this application among the best.

[1] Career objective belongs in cover letter, not the resume.

[2] Is this the same as a major or was there none? Perhaps applicant had a double major—management and finance.

[3] Since there is no reference to academic achievement, the assumption is there was none.

[4] Very, very strong business experience.

[5] Unique life experience—solid overseas business experience.

[6] Because none of these interests relate to the type of position applied for, inclusion is unnecessary.

[7] Hype. Lends no real value.

[8] It is not necessary to include this information.

RESUME FIVE

HOME: SCHOOL:

EDUCATION

The University of Texas at Austin
Bachelor of Business Administration-Finance,
May 1996

[1]   Finance GPA 4.0/4.0   Overall GPA 3.63/4.0

[2] **EXPERIENCE**

Sept. 1995-   **Financial Institutions Committee**, Texas House of
Dec. 1995   Representatives, Austin, Texas
                Intern; Bill-Research and Analysis
[3]   Ashley Smith, Chairman; Financial Institutions
[4]   Committee: (512) 463-0696
                                         (12 hrs. per week)

Aug. 1993-   **Sterling C. Evans Library**, Texas A&M University,
March 1995   College Station, Texas
                Student Assistant in Reference &
                Circulation Departments
[4]   Circulation Dept.: (409) 845-3731
                                         (up to 24 hrs. per week)

May 1992-   **Cooks Night Out**, New York Style Deli, Austin, Texas
Aug. 1992   Counter Clerk, food preparation, and pastry cook
                                         (30 hrs. per week)

[5] **Honors &**
Activities   Dean's Honor Role, Fall 1995 (University of Texas)
                Dean's Honor Role, Fall 1993 (Texas A&M University)   [7]
[6]   Volunteer, Austin Nature Center, Spring 1996
                University of Texas Finance Association, 1995-1996
                Texas A&M Finance Association, 1994-1995
                Texas A&M Pre-Law Association, 1994-1995
                Volunteer, Junior Helping Hand Home for Children,
                    Spring 1994
                Assistant Chairman, Haunted House Fund-raiser for
                    Off-Campus Aggies
                Member, Texas A&M Boxing Club, 1993-1994
                Member, Phi Kappa Sigma Fraternity, 1992-1995

[5]   Special Skills

- Knowledge of many spreadsheets and word   **[8]**
  processors
- Strong interpersonal and communication skills
- Excellent research and reference skills
- Work extremely well under pressure
- Team player with experience in group projects

[5]   References

Johnny Johnson	(214) 754-1780
Rep. Ashley Smith	(512) 463-0696 **[9]**
Charles Betts	(512) 480-8200

CRITIQUING THE RESUME

RESUME FIVE

EXPERIENCE RATER

	Points
College Attended	3
Courses of Study	5
Academic Achievement	5
Extracurricular Activities	3
Work Experience	1
Unique Life Experience	0
Total	17

Experience Rating:	Very Good

Comment: Strong academic record. I want to know why he left one school after his junior year to attend and graduate from another. No summer work in 1993 and 1995 and possibly none in 1994. No cover letter included, and thus we have no idea of his job objective. Makes resume nearly worthless.

[1] Normally, only the best grade point average is included. However, when more than one GPA is outstanding, both can be noted.

[2] Experience should be Employment Experience.

[3] Working for a state representative is an excellent resume asset. Note work was part time.

[4] For some reason, applicant included phone numbers for these activities. Their inclusion is unnecessary on a resume.

[5] Headings should be all capital to be equal in weight to Education and Experience.

[6] While list of activities is varied, there aren't any leadership positions. Applicant seems to have strong social work interests.

[7] Honor Role at two schools is impressive but spelling of "Role" is not.

[8] Evaluatory adjectives tend to oversell. Stating skills without adjectives is ethically more acceptable. This section is more hype than deed.

[9] It is okay to include references if one or more is impressive. Such was the case here.

RESUME SIX

Present Address   **Permanent Address**

Objective: To gain technical knowledge and experience in the financial world.

EDUCATION:

Brandeis University, Waltham, MA
B.A. in Economics, Cum Laude; May 1996

Studies include: International Trade Theory; Financial Theory; Russian Economics; The Firm in the International Economy; The Economics of Technological Change; General Psychology; Sociology of Birth and Death; Calculus; Sculpture; Contemporary Painting and Sculpture

Syracuse University Program in Florence, Florence, Italy
Spring Semester 1995

SKILLS:

Fluent in Spanish.
Proficient in Italian and French.
Working knowledge of D-base, Lotus 1-2-3, and WordPerfect.

EXPERIENCE:

PEER COUNSELING HOTLINE	Brandeis University
Counselor	1993–1996

Participated in four paraprofessional training sessions designed to refine counseling skills. Counsel peers on suicide, rape, relationship problems, eating disorders, and other topics, while remaining anonymous and confidential.

Co-Coordinator   Fall 1994

Programmed and directed over 100 hours of training on counseling skills, and other topics. Arranged for set-up of office, phone service, referral and reference materials. Appointed committee members and monitored committee activities. Planned and supervised meetings.

WENNIGER GRAPHICS GALLERY   Boston, MA
Intern, Assistant to Manager   Fall 1995
Advertised shows to media and public via
telephone and mail campaigns. Sold art work.
Created displays. Interacted with customers
and artists.

STATE FARM INSURANCE   Houston, TX
Secretary   Summer 1995
Centralized communications between field agents
and various storm offices. Oversaw the closing of
two storm offices. Provided general office support
services.

THE METHODIST HOSPITAL CORPORATION   Houston, TX
Management Systems Consulting   Summer 1994
Department Intern
Collaborated with consultants regarding
recommendations and revisions for projects
and reports. Implemented plan to computerize
research library for department.

L.B. KUDISCH AND A. WERCH, P.A.   Houston, TX
Receptionist   1988–1992
Balanced patient accounts. Filed insurance
forms. Interacted with patients and doctors. Billed
patients for services.

AWARDS:

GIRL SCOUT GOLD AWARD: Equivalent to the   Houston, TX
Boy Scout Eagle Scout. Discovered a need in   1992
the community to educate various universities,
businesses, and companies on the merits of the
Gold Award and its recipients.

RESUME PERSONAL CRITIQUE

RESUME SIX

Instructions: This is an opportunity for you to critique an actual resume. Before you do, try to rate it on the Experience Rater (page 30) and assign it a related Experience Rating. I have identified six items worth noting from the resume. After you have completed your critique, turn to the next page and compare it with mine.

EXPERIENCE RATER

	Points
College Attended	____
Courses of Study	____
Academic Achievement	____
Extracurricular Activities	____
Work Experience	____
Unique Life Experience	____
Total	

Experience Rating: _____

Comment: _____

_____

_____

_____

[1] _____

_____

[2] _____

_____

[3] _____

_____

[4] _____

_____

[5] _____

_____

[6] _____

_____

RESUME SIX

Present Address   **Permanent Address**

[1]   <u>Objective:</u> To gain technical knowledge and experience in the financial world.

EDUCATION:

Brandeis University, Waltham, MA
[2]   <u>B.A. in Economics, Cum Laude; May 1996</u>

[3]   <u>Studies include: International Trade Theory; Financial Theory;
Russian Economics; The Firm in the International Economy;
The Economics of Technological Change; General Psychology;
Sociology of Birth and Death; Calculus; Sculpture; Contemporary
Painting and Sculpture</u>

[4]   **<u>Syracuse University Program in Florence</u>**<u>, Florence, Italy
Spring Semester 1995</u>

SKILLS:

Fluent in Spanish.
Proficient in Italian and French.
[5]   <u>Working knowledge of D-base, Lotus 1-2-3, and WordPerfect.</u>

EXPERIENCE:

		Brandeis
[6]	<u>PEER COUNSELING HOTLINE</u>	University
	Counselor	1993–1996

Participated in four paraprofessional training
sessions designed to refine counseling skills.
Counsel peers on suicide, rape, relationship
problems, eating disorders, and other topics,
while remaining anonymous and confidential.

Co-Coordinator   Fall 1994

Programmed and directed over 100 hours of
training on counseling skills, and other topics.
Arranged for set-up of office, phone service,
referral and reference materials. Appointed
committee members and monitored committee
activities. Planned and supervised meetings.

WENNIGER GRAPHICS GALLERY   Boston, MA
Intern, Assistant to Manager   Fall 1995
Advertised shows to media and public via
telephone and mail campaigns. Sold art work.
Created displays. Interacted with customers
and artists.

STATE FARM INSURANCE   Houston, TX
Secretary   Summer 1995
Centralized communications between field agents
and various storm offices. Oversaw the closing of
two storm offices. Provided general office support
services.

THE METHODIST HOSPITAL CORPORATION   Houston, TX
Management Systems Consulting   Summer 1994
Department Intern
Collaborated with consultants regarding
recommendations and revisions for projects and
reports. Implemented plan to computerize
research library for department.

L.B. KUDISCH AND A. WERCH, P.A.   Houston, TX
Receptionist   1988–1992
Balanced patient accounts. Filed insurance
forms. Interacted with patients and doctors. Billed
patients for services.

AWARDS:

[4]   **<u>GIRL SCOUT GOLD AWARD:</u>** Equivalent to the   Houston, TX
         Boy Scout Eagle Scout. Discovered a need in   1992
         the community to educate various universities,
         businesses, and companies on the merits of the
         Gold Award and its recipients.

CRITIQUING THE RESUME

RESUME SIX

EXPERIENCE RATER

	Points
College Attended	3
Courses of Study	3
Academic Achievement	3
Extracurricular Activities	0
Work Experience	5
Unique Life Experience	5
Total	19

Experience Rating: Outstanding

Comment: This resume shows strong academic leanings to the business world, but equally strong characteristics in the social work arena. It would be difficult to hire someone with such diverse interests. Applicant has very broad assets—computer, international, social work, languages, office administration, and so on—but where does she fit?

[1] Not only is the job objective unnecessary here, it is badly stated since it is so self-serving. She is looking for knowledge and experience, not a career of contributing to the progress of a company.

[2] With a cum laude designation, why wasn't the grade point average included?

[3] Many of these subjects don't relate well to the financial world (sculpture, painting, etc.). Why include them?

[4] Unique life experiences.

[5] Question: Are you better served by naming the specific software you are experienced in or by stating more generally that you are proficient in several?

[6] Was Peer Counseling Hotline a paid position or an extracurricular activity?

14. Writing the Cover Letter

Now that we have constructed an outstanding resume, what do we do for an encore? In order to properly transmit the resume to prospective employers, the resume is, in most cases, accompanied by a cover letter. Consequently, the next step in the chase for great job interviews is to create and use a good cover letter.

The cover letter has two functions. Its primary purpose is to introduce the resume. Employers generally do not read, and rarely respond to, a resume received without an accompanying cover letter. Lacking a cover letter gives the impression of an incomplete effort by the applicant—a very quick turn-off.

A cover letter is not, however, required in all situations. For example, if someone asks for a copy of your resume, a cover letter is not needed but can be included. If you decide to pass out your resume to friends and family, a cover letter is not required. If someone invites you in for an interview, it may also be unnecessary. But in the vast majority of cases, a cover letter is mandatory because it serves to introduce the resume.

The cover letter has a second function—to stimulate the interviewer to read your resume. Remember, the resume is the selling document, but if it doesn't get read, it won't sell for you. The cover letter must focus the employer's attention on the resume, not on itself. Later in this chapter, we will explore how that can best be accomplished.

Let's begin by constructing an excellent cover letter. The best cover letter consists of four parts:

1. Purpose of the letter
2. Your job objective
3. One or two key resume items
4. Action follow-up

The contents of a cover letter should be contained in just three paragraphs. If the cover letter is too long, the reader will lose interest and be less inclined to read the resume (which is, you'll recall, the purpose of the cover letter). But, if it is too short, it won't have enough content to stimulate the employer to read the resume either.

Let's continue our mission of getting Bob Wilson a lot of great interviews by constructing his mythical cover letter.

The *first paragraph* of his letter should state why the letter is being written—in other words, what the goal of the sender is. The goal is always to obtain an interview with the company, not to secure a job with that firm. That comes later. Here's an example of his opening paragraph:

> As you will see in the enclosed resume, I have devoted much of my Decatur College undergraduate time preparing for the accounting profession. The purpose of this letter is to arrange an interview with you to discuss employment with Maxwell and Associates.

Simple, positive, and to the point. It tells the interviewer the letter's purpose without asking her to plod through endless prose. If you are fortunate enough to have an introduction to the interviewer, it should appear as the first sentence. Here is a sample lead-in sentence:

> Mr. William Rodgers of ABC Company has suggested I contact you. As you will see in the enclosed resume, . . .

The *second paragraph* should state the job objective:

> Specifically, I am seeking a position as an accountant with your firm. Although my preference is for a position in your Corporate Department, alternative accounting opportunities would be considered.

The main question that needs to be addressed in this paragraph is, "How specific should the job objective be?" If you know exactly what you want to do, your job objective can be very specific—employers appreciate that. If you are less certain of what you want to do or are unsure how the company structures its positions, you can state the job objective more generally. A drawback in being specific with the job objective is that the interviewing company may not have an opening in that area but might in a related department. If the job objective is too narrow, you may not be offered an opportunity to interview for a related position.

Emphasize Strong Assets

Following the job objective, but still in the second paragraph, is the opportunity to emphasize one or two of your resume's strongest points. This is the key part of the cover letter. Remember, its sole function is to stimulate the interviewer to read your resume. Selection of the resume items to include in the cover letter is critical because they can either encourage further review of your credentials or reduce your chances significantly.

To be effective in the cover letter, the strongest resume asset(s) must have two characteristics. First, the item(s) selected must relate as closely as possible to the position, industry, or company you are pursuing. If you are applying for an accounting job, there is little to be gained in the cover letter in pointing out that you were an all-conference wide receiver on the football team or that you were your fraternity's social chairman. On the other hand, you will advance your cause significantly if you note that you have been named a top accounting student. The cover letter's selling point(s) should relate closely to the position being sought.

Second, the resume item to be cited in the cover letter should be something that positions you above your peer group. In our example, it would not be particularly effective to say you are a member of your school's accounting society even though that association relates directly to the position you are seeking. Activities of this sort are generally open to anyone who wants to join them. Membership usually requires no distinction. If, however, you were elected president of the accounting society, you will have a powerful asset to show a prospective employer, because it implies both significant dedication to accounting and strong leadership characteristics—desirable qualities that set you apart from your peers and projects you as an above-average candidate. Along the same line, a grade point average of 3.1, while good, is not good enough to be included in the cover letter. A 3.8 average would be.

The continuation of the second paragraph of Wilson's cover letter can look like this:

> While at Decatur, I was a three-year member of the Accounting Society and was elected its Chairman in my senior year. I also achieved a grade point average of 3.8 in my accounting subjects while in school. Additional college achievements are included in the enclosed resume.

An interviewer for an accounting firm would certainly be impressed by these credentials and would undoubtedly review the resume.

Action Paragraph

The *third paragraph* is the action paragraph—the what-happens-next section. In this section, the applicant informs the interviewer he will be contacting him by phone in a few days. The letter concludes with a general thank you in the third paragraph and, by implication, urges the employer to review the resume. Here is how it looks:

> Within a few days, I will call you to arrange an appropriate time to meet at your convenience. Thank you for reviewing my resume.

It is very important not to conclude your cover letter by asking the employers to contact you if they have an interest. It would be wonderful if employers did respond to cover letters and resumes, but it doesn't often happen. Most interviewers don't have the time to reply to all applicants, and they often have too many applicants to choose from. I've had one interviewer tell me he never responds to a resume. He wants to see who has the gumption to call him. Follow up every cover letter with a prompt call or the application can falter.

Let's put the three paragraphs together and see how they look as a completed letter:

147 Arkansas Street
Albuquerque, NM 87110
February 15, 1996

Mr. Robert Arnold, President
Maxwell and Associates
143 South Hill Street
Lamborn, NY 10542

Dear Mr. Arnold:

As you will see in the enclosed resume, I have devoted much of my Decatur College undergraduate time preparing for the accounting profession. The purpose of this letter is to arrange an interview with you to discuss employment with Maxwell and Associates.

Specifically, I am seeking a position as an accountant with your firm. Although my preference is for a position in your Corporate Department, alternative accounting opportunities would be considered. While at Decatur, I was a three-year member of the Accounting Society and was elected its Chairman in my senior year. I also achieved a grade point average of 3.8 in my accounting subjects while in school. Additional college achievements are included in the enclosed resume.

Within a few days, I will call you to arrange an appropriate time to meet at your convenience. Thank you for reviewing my resume.

Sincerely yours,

Robert G. Wilson

This letter will get attention. Of course, not every firm you pursue will have an entry-level accounting position opening, but if they do, this cover letter will get your resume reviewed.

Before we leave the cover letter, let's highlight a few additional points. You often see cover letters that contain qualitative judgments of an applicant's characteristics. Here are three that are representative:

1. I am a responsible, energetic student . . .
2. My work experience and extracurricular activities have provided me with the essential interpersonal skills and leadership experience I feel are necessary ingredients for success in today's competitive environment.
3. I have the ability, dependability, enthusiasm, and determination to assist your firm . . .

This kind of self-evaluation in a cover letter is of no value. It is virtually impossible for someone who is twenty-one years old to know what it takes to succeed in business. The cultures simply are too far apart. Remember, the interviewer is far more interested in your accomplishments than in your self-evaluation. Stick to the facts—deeds always speak louder than hype.

The cover letter can advance your cause or stop it in its tracks. It depends on its contents. Here are some characteristics of the cover letter that can work against you. I call them the "Seven Cover Letter Don'ts." Let's take a look, and remember to avoid them in your cover letter.

The Seven Cover Letter Don'ts

1. **Don't overuse the word "I." It's very difficult to write a cover letter without using the word "I," yet a cover letter containing many "I"s will not be well received by the reader. Recently I received a cover letter with twelve "I"s. In addition, it contained six "my"s and "me"s—a total of eighteen references to the writer. Needless to say, I rejected the inquiry believing, perhaps incorrectly, that the applicant was too self-centered to be suitable for the available position. I never found out if I was wrong because the applicant didn't get a chance to prove otherwise.**
2. **Don't write a long cover letter. Be brief. Interviewers will not plod through a long cover letter. In business, every effort is made to communicate effectively—that is, briefly and to the point. A lengthy letter is an indication that the applicant cannot effectively and efficiently transmit a message.**
3. **Don't make any grammatical mistakes. College graduates are**

assumed to know correct English. Nonetheless, I have seen some pretty poor grammar in cover letters. Nothing turns off an interviewer more than a letter containing poor grammar, spelling, or punctuation. How many times have we heard that college graduates don't know how to write? Often enough to counsel that a cover letter with poor grammar can void an outstanding resume. To eliminate grammatical weaknesses, have all cover letters reviewed and proofread by an educated person before they are mailed.

4. Don't rehash the resume. As mentioned earlier, include one or two key resume points in the cover letter to entice the employer to read the resume. Leave something in the resume for the interviewer to get further excited about. Remember, the resume is the selling document; the cover letter simply introduces it.

5. Don't fill the cover letter with meaningless prose or flowery praise such as, "After careful research, I have determined that Maxwell and Associates is among the best accounting firms in the business, and I would like to be associated with a top company such as yours." Unless Maxwell and Associates is among the best accounting firms, this type of praise falls short of the mark. In fact, it can be a negative if the interviewer knows it isn't true. Another overstated comment: "Maxwell and Associates offers the type of employment and advancement opportunities I seek." There is no way you would know that—thus it is worthless prose. Stick to the basics.

6. Don't oversell in the cover letter. When applicants attempt to sell themselves through words rather than deeds, they lose the interviewer, who knows that form of selling is worthless. Selling is done in the resume, which recounts the applicant's achievements and successes. Further, if you use all of your selling points in the cover letter, you'll have nothing new in the resume to entice the employer into an interview.

7. Don't indicate in your job objective that you are seeking a position in which you can learn (train, become educated) about the business. Employers would rather have applicants that are going to be productive. The company expects to train new employees, but that's not why they hire them.

Letters Critiqued

On the following pages, you will see graphic reviews of actual cover letters, pointing out their strong and weak points. As you review the cover letters, look for the bracketed numbers and the corresponding underlined portions of each cover letter. Then match them with the explanation in the "CRITIQUING THE COVER LETTER" section following each cover letter. The five letters that follow are critiqued both as to their overall qualities—how they get the job done—and their specific content, both good and bad. While most inadequacies are noted, some are not due to space limitations or because we have made prior reference to them.

The evaluation of Cover Letter Six is blank. This will give you an opportunity to test your skills in critiquing a cover letter. So that you can measure your success, I have completed a critique of Letter Six on the page following it.

When you have finished your review of these cover letters, you will see that the critiques emphasize:

1. Grammar and punctuation
2. Hype—it's unnecessary
3. Concentration on citing strong selling points
4. Brevity—keep it short
5. Follow-up phone calls
6. Overcomplimenting target companies

As an individual beginning your first full-time job search, it is very important that your cover letter (and resume) be reviewed by a knowledgeable, educated person. The inadequacies of the letters that follow could have been avoided with a careful review.

LETTER ONE

1400 Clarewood   [1]
Abilene, TX 79604
915/392-4831

[2]   Dear Branch Manager,

I have acquainted myself with Morgan Securities and I am extremely
interested in a <u>prolonged career</u> as a stockbroker. I am seeking a bro-   [3]
kerage position with your firm because I feel that I have the necessary
qualifications to do an outstanding job for your firm, while learning the
basic components of your needs. I selected your firm because <u>it is an</u>
<u>outstanding member of the brokerage community and a recognized</u>   [4]
<u>leader in broker training</u>, which I recognize as essential to <u>maintain</u>   [5]
your present status. I have studied the basic background of the brokerage industry, and <u>I am deeply interested in furthering my knowledge,</u> to   [6]
the benefit of your firm. I would like to apply my genuine enthusiasm
towards your firm as a stockbroker trainee.

In order to finance my college education, I took on jobs where my com-
[7]   pensation was based largely upon my <u>performance</u>, this <u>gives</u> me a   [8]
firm foundation for obtaining results with cost and schedule constraints
under pressures to "produce or perish." My accomplishments in each
job were acknowledged by substantial salary increases.

[9]   <u>Serving as a leader in many different roles in my college fraternity</u>
required honesty, tact, and initiative. These qualities will be an
important part of my code of ethics as a stockbroker.

My background includes sales and practical market knowledge through
the AT&T Collegiate Investment Challenge, as well as a variety of business courses in school, which I believe would <u>benefit my contribution to</u>   [10]
<u>your firm</u>. By conducting a personal interview, you will be able to form a
more complete idea of my personality and drive to succeed, as well as
the many unique ways I can benefit your firm.

After you've had time to review my application and resume, will you
[11]   please <u>call or write me</u> at the above address or telephone number.
Thank you for your time and consideration.

                                        Sincerely,

                                        Christopher M. Davis

Enclosure: Resume

CRITIQUING THE COVER LETTER

LETTER ONE

REVIEW COMMENTS

The cover letter is too long—five paragraphs. It's loaded with hype and tends to oversell with verbiage rather than results. Nothing in the letter is exciting enough to encourage reading the resume.

NOTE COMMENTS
---

[1] No date on letter.

[2] Should be addressed to a specific person. It would have been easy to get the correct name.

[3] "prolonged career" is superfluous.

[4] There is no way the applicant can be sure the firm "is an outstanding member of the brokerage community" or "a recognized leader in broker training."

[5] "maintain" should be maintaining.

[6] Employers are not interested in an applicant's goal of furthering his knowledge.

[7] Sentence should end with "performance." "This" would start a new sentence.

[8] "gives" should be gave.

[9] Applicant's resume showed no such positions.

[10] What does "benefit my contribution to your firm" mean?

[11] Always indicate applicant will follow up with a phone call, especially for budding salespeople.

LETTER TWO

2515 Leon Street
Dallas, TX 75230
214/761-8921
September 3, 1996

Ms. Tonya McLain
P.O. Box 1756
Edmond, OK 73003

[1]   Tonya:

Enclosed is a copy of my resume for your viewing pleasure.   [2]
[3]   Understand that I am very interested in the opportunities your firm
[4]   have to offer. Crews & Associates has been a very adequate firm to   [5]
learn and grow. Obviously I have higher ambitions than a colonial   [6]
[2]   house, picket fence, and a dog.

[7]   One idea of concern is instability in my work history. I hold no   [5]
remorse in the decisions that I have made thus far. At each turn in the   [2]
road, I have learned a great many things that can only benefit my   [8]
future. My current age is 22 years old (or young). It is time to seek a   [2]
company that I can grow with and be assured that however the market
turns, management will keep an open mind to new products.   [9]

I appreciate the opportunity to speak with you, and am excited about
[10]   pursuing this in greater detail. Your enthusiasm leads me to believe   [11]
[11]   that you are also open minded. This also encourages me to the fact
that your firm could hold future possibilities.

Thank you,

Donna R. Forsyth

CRITIQUING THE COVER LETTER

LETTER TWO

REVIEW COMMENTS

Frankly, this is a bad letter. There is absolutely nothing in the letter to entice an employer's interest. It is far too chatty and familiar, and it has a definite negative thrust. There are too many mistakes to comment on them all.

NOTE COMMENTS

---

[1] Never address a business letter to a stranger using their first name, as was done here.

[2] Clichés such as "viewing pleasure," "colonial house, picket fence, and a dog," "at each turn in the road," "22 years old (or young)" are totally unacceptable.

[3] Sentence strangely constructed. It sounds like an order.

[4] "have" should be "has."

[5] Negatives such as "very adequate firm to learn and grow," "instability in my work history," "I hold no remorse" are very unsatisfactory.

[6] Why obviously?

[7] Whose concern—applicant's or company's?

[8] "benefit my future" should be "benefit me in the future."

[9] What do new products have to do with a job application?

[10] What is "this"?

[11] How do enthusiasm and open-mindedness relate?

LETTER THREE

4000 Dolphin Street
Macon, GA 31210
912/560-4821
April 30, 1996

Robert Brown
Retail Division Recruiting
Harrison Securities, Inc.
P.O. Box 508
Dallas, TX 75221

Dear Mr. Brown,

[1]   "Choose a career you enjoy and learn everything from the ground
up. Don't be afraid to get your hands dirty and with hard work, success
is a lock." This quote has motivated me to achieve several of my goals   [2]
except one, which is a career in the securities and investment industry.

       The purpose of this letter is to inquire about your an entry level posi-   [3]
[4]   tion in your retail division. In December, I graduated from St. Mary's
University in San Antonio, Texas, with a B.B.A. in Marketing. As a
[5]   campus leader and a student-athlete on scholarship, I have developed
[6]   the competitive attitude and interpersonal skills that you are looking for.
As a result, I feel that I can utilize these skills to complement your sales
force.

       Enclosed is my resume that provides additional information on my
undergraduate activities and work experience. Even though I do not   [7]
have previous experience in the securities and investments industry
that you usually look for, I believe that I will continue to be a success at
whatever I put my mind to. I would like the opportunity to meet with you
to discuss how I can contribute to your company. I look forward to   [8]
hearing from you.

                          Sincerely,

                          Robert M. Godschalk

CRITIQUING THE COVER LETTER

LETTER THREE

REVIEW COMMENTS

This is a relatively decent letter, starting with the creative opening, which is an interesting gamble. While the letter has significant flaws, it is concise and somewhat enticing. I think I'd read further.

NOTE COMMENTS
---

[1] Creative opening but it doesn't necessarily advance the applicant's cause.

[2] "several" should be "all."

[3] The word "your" is superfluous.

[4] Avoid showing in the cover letter that four months have passed since graduation. Interviewers will wonder why applicant is still looking for a job. Replace "In December" with "Recently."

[5] This section encourages the interviewer to find out how much of a campus leader and student athlete the applicant was. The resume should be read.

[6] Hype.

[7] Negative point—why include it? It will be apparent in the resume but by then other assets may overcome it.

[8] No indication of follow-up call.

LETTER FOUR

January 21, 1996

[1]   Mrs. Roberta Ackles
Roberts Smith, Inc.
Corporate Intern (2-year program)
1725 Maple Street
Havertown, PA 19083

Dear Mrs. Ackles:

The Mexican Peso devaluation, interest rate volatility, and the Federal
Government deficit could make some recent Business School gradu-   [2]
ates a little pessimistic about employment prospects. I choose to be
very optimistic. Now more than ever firms that were able to survive the   [4]
[3]   economic downturn of recent years need to be ready to benefit from
the market when it cycles upwards again. Enthusiastic new employees
will be needed to solve the complex issues arising from today's
competitive business environment.

You are probably asking yourself where such an employee can be
obtained. Of course, I would suggest a recent college graduate in
[3]   finance from one of the top twenty Business Schools in the country   [2]
such as the University of Texas at Austin, but I am somewhat biased.

If you will review my resume, you will find that I just happen to be such
a graduate. I have a substantial amount of experience working in a
[3]   professional environment with a high degree of responsibility, and I
have paid for 100% of my college expenses. I am also computer
literate with many software packages.

I am attracted to the Corporate Intern Program because it offers a   [5]
dynamic opportunity to train in an intensive high responsibility and high
profile position. I understand that the position does not begin until June,   [6]
but I would like to learn more about it now. I would like to set up an   [7]
interview with you to discuss this program and to show you my
qualifications.

[8]   Thankyou very much for your time. I will call later this week to learn   [9]
more about opportunities at Roberts Smith, Inc., or I can be reached at
(214) 671-0859.

Sincerely,

Evelyn K. Ferrara

Resume Enclosed

CRITIQUING THE COVER LETTER

LETTER FOUR

REVIEW COMMENTS

It's hard to have a strong position on this letter. On the one hand, it's creative; on the other, it's hype. Moreover, the first half seems a bit negative. A letter like this is a gamble—some interviewers simply won't plow through the rhetoric. The letter is too long and includes no return address.

NOTE COMMENTS

---

[1] Roberta Ackles is unmarried. Applicant makes a big mistake being wrong on this issue. Ms. is correct when you are not positive.

[2] Business School should not be capitalized unless it is part of a school's title.

[3] The opening three paragraphs are a little too "smart." The beginning simply doesn't advance the cause.

[4] Comma needed between "ever" and "firms."

[5] How does applicant know this? Furthermore, a business firm's primary goal in hiring new employees is for them to be productive, not to be educated.

[6] It is very difficult to know what position the candidate is seeking. There is no indication of her desire.

[7] Letter contains thirteen "I"s—too many.

[8] "Thankyou" should have a space— "Thank you."

[9] Good finish.

LETTER FIVE

10601 Mills Circle
Mobile, AL 36608
May 31, 1996

Ms. Lynn Mellor
Assistant Manager - Personnel
Coleman Financial Inc.
595 Madison Avenue
New York, NY 10010

Dear Ms. Mellor,

[1]   I read your company's profile in the University of Texas at Arlington
(UTA) and would like to inquire about employment opportunities as a
stockbroker or any other suitable positions currently available. I am   [2]
interested in providing and selling a wide range of investment services
to individual investors as well as corporations.

My BBA is in Finance from UTA. The degree plan required additional   [3]
[4]   courses in Investments, Financial Institutions and Markets, Financial
Management of Financial Institutions, and International Corporate
Finance. These courses provide an excellent foundation for entering the
financial investments industry. Besides possessing technical skills, I am
also able to speak three different languages. Furthermore, I have gained   [5]
[7]   valuable experience working as a Resident Assistant at the University.
Supervising residence halls and administering university policies have
improved my communication skills and skills in managing people.
Moreover, my extensive involvement in the various leadership activities
[6]   in University demonstrates my strong motivation to succeed. In addition,
I am also very ambitious as well as hardworking. Enclosed is a copy of
my resume which expands on my background and qualifications.

Please consider my request for a personal interview to discuss my
qualifications and interests. Thank you for your time and consideration.
[8]   I look forward to talking with you soon.

Sincerely,

Milton Kim

Enclosure: Resume

CRITIQUING THE COVER LETTER

LETTER FIVE

REVIEW COMMENTS

While flawed in a number of ways, this letter is still a reasonably good one. Heavy emphasis placed on specific achievements is the major plus. I believe I would read the resume.

NOTE COMMENTS
---

[1] "in" should be "at."

[2] How dedicated is the applicant to being a stockbroker if he is willing to consider "any other suitable positions"?

[3] "additional" is unnecessary and confusing.

[4] If appropriate at all, a list of courses is more suited to the resume. In this case, the courses described are not perfect for a stockbroker's position, so nothing is gained by including them.

[5] Solid enticement on several levels—speaks three languages, resident advisor position, leadership activities—encourages reader to review resume.

[6] "in" should be "at the."

[7] Second paragraph is too long. It should have been two paragraphs or shortened.

[8] No reference to follow-up call.

LETTER SIX

10024 Regal Park Lane
Ridgewood, NJ 07043
February 26, 1996

Micheal W. Moore
Vice President Recruiting and Training
Williams & Co.
740 Broadway
San Diego, CA 92037

Dear Mr. Moore,

I am writing you to inquire about an entry level position with your firm. I am interested in public finance, research, and fixed income trading. I would like to stress some aspects of my personality and background which make me an ideal candidate for your company.

After having studied theoretical economics at Brandeis University I am eager to learn more about the technical aspects of finance and investment analysis. I would like to start at an entry level position in which I would assume responsibility quickly. I have strong analytical and problem solving abilities. My ability to work with people in various contexts will be helpful to your company.

A copy of my resume is enclosed for your review. I would like to meet with you to discuss the possibilities of our working together. I will call you in a week to ten days to set up an appointment. If you have any questions please contact me at 987-3269.

Yours truly,

Harry Schultz

COVER LETTER PERSONAL CRITIQUE

LETTER SIX

Instructions: On the preceding page is an actual cover letter. You are invited to critique it yourself. I have found ten items I believe are worth noting. You might also care to make some review comments. Ask yourself if the contents of the cover letter are interesting enough to induce you to make a careful review of the resume. When your critique is concluded, check the next page to see how it compares with mine.

REVIEW COMMENTS

NOTE COMMENTS

---

[1] _____

[2] _____

_____

[3] _____

[4] _____

_____

[5] _____

[6] _____

_____

[7] _____

[8] _____

_____

[9] _____

_____

[10] _____

_____

LETTER SIX

10024 Regal Park Lane
Ridgewood, NJ 07043
February 26, 1996

[1]   <u>Micheal</u> W. Moore
Vice President Recruiting and Training
Williams & Co.
740 Broadway
San Diego, CA 92037

Dear Mr. Moore,

[2]   <u>I</u> am writing you to inquire about an entry level position with your
firm. I am interested in <u>public finance, research, and fixed income</u>   [3]
[4]   <u>trading</u>. I would like to <u>stress</u> some aspects of my personality and   [5]
background which make me an ideal candidate for your company.

        After having studied theoretical economics at Brandeis <u>University</u>   [6]
[7]   I am <u>eager to learn</u> more about the technical aspects of finance and
investment analysis. I would like to start at an entry level position in
which I would assume responsibility quickly. I have strong analytical
and problem solving abilities. <u>My ability to work with people in various</u>   [8]
<u>contexts will be helpful to your company</u>.

[9]   A copy of my resume is enclosed for your review. <u>I would like to</u>
<u>meet with you to discuss the possibilities of our working together</u>. <u>I will</u>
<u>call you in a week to ten days to set up an appointment</u>. If you have
any questions please contact me at <u>987-3269</u>.   [10]

                        Yours truly,

                        Harry Schultz

CRITIQUING THE COVER LETTER

LETTER SIX

REVIEW COMMENTS

While this isn't a bad letter, it isn't great. Most of the content is too general. Remember, deeds sell much better than verbiage. Indicating that the applicant will call for an appointment is a positive—should be included in every letter.

NOTE COMMENTS

---

[1] Micheal should be spelled Michael.

[2] Letter has too many references to "I," "me," or "my"—fourteen in all.

[3] Applicant shows three dissimilar fields of interest. This implies applicant is unsure of his direction.

[4] This sentence should start the second paragraph because it pertains to information that follows it.

[5] "emphasize" is a much better word than "stress" in this situation.

[6] A comma is needed between "University" and "I."

[7] Employers are not interested in an applicant's interest in learning. They would prefer applicant emphasize productivity possibilities.

[8] How does applicant know his ability to work with people would be helpful to the company?

[9] Excellent plan and a good way to close letter except the follow-up call should be made sooner.

[10] Phone number should include area code.

15. Unique Applications

Every year, applications for employment deluge employers. Virtually all consist of a cover letter and a resume. It is an enormously difficult process to review each one fairly and render an impartial evaluation.

It is a fact that all applicants are not treated equally. Timing, for example, is a key ingredient in whether an applicant gets properly reviewed. The day of the week that an application is received, surprisingly, can be a factor in how carefully it is evaluated. More importantly, is the application received at a time when a job is available? How many times have we heard this comment, "If only I had known of your interest earlier. I just filled a job for which you appear to be qualified." There are so many subtle aspects to the timing of the application that one wonders about the whole process. Even the time of day a resume lands on an interviewer's desk can have a bearing on how it gets handled.

All of this leads to a discussion of whether there is a way to make an application demand review by the interviewer. Some job seekers create unique applications in the hope that they will receive greater attention. The unique application is fraught with risk and is more often inappropriate than appropriate. Ultimately, you are judged on your merits anyway. The argument advanced by those who submit unique applications is that they are more likely to be read and there is some truth to that.

Why Prepare a Unique Application?
1. **Quickly grabs attention—thus more likely to be read.**
2. **Projects the personality of the applicant.**
3. **Sets the applicant apart from the competition.**
4. **Permits an individualized approach.**

As you might guess, there is a delicate balance between a resume that is unique and one that goes overboard. For example, if you are applying for a position as an engineer with a major corporation, a unique application may not receive serious attention. If you are applying for a position in the creative department of an advertising company, however, a standard approach might not be interesting enough to stand out among all the creative applications the interviewer might receive. So a decision on whether a creative approach should be used to a great extent depends on the type of position being sought. An application that is too unique for the job will often be looked upon negatively.

> *Your application should demand*
> *attention from the interviewer.*

Perhaps the best way to address the subject is to describe some of the unique applications that interview seekers use. On the surface, the approaches described here will seem "off the wall" because they are, in fact, out of the ordinary. The decision to use a unique approach must be carefully reasoned. If in doubt, don't use it.

A unique application may be nothing more than a resume on colored paper. Although almost all resumes are on white paper, those printed on light gray paper, for example, could stand out. In the same vein, resumes are usually on one sheet of 8½-by-11-inch paper. Why not submit one on 8½-by-11-inch paper folded in half and printed like a book? This would certainly remove the resume from the ordinary.

A Cut Above

One job applicant I know always clipped a one-inch triangular slice from the upper righthand corner of her resume, cover letter, and all later correspondence. An interviewer would certainly take notice of this unusual approach. When asked why the resume and the cover letter were cut in the upper righthand corner, the applicant said that she wanted to get across to the interviewer that her application was "a cut above" the competition. On the thank you notes following her interviews, she continued her "cut above" theme.

Personalizing an application is not unusual and can create an element of interest. Personalization is essentially handwriting a sentence or two in ink on the cover letter. The handwritten sentence could be as simple as, "Mr. Jones, I would welcome the opportunity to discuss the oil industry with you." Or, it can be personalized further if you have had actual contact with the interviewer in the past. Personalization takes your application out of the ordinary. Make sure your handwriting is extremely legible, otherwise it will become a negative.

A Sales Letter Instead

Another unique approach involves eliminating the cover letter and resume and substituting a sales letter in their place. A sales letter contains several of your strongest assets organized in a selling fashion. It normally starts with a one-sentence description of a significant accomplishment such as, "In my most recent summer employment, I made an average of thirty-five calls a day for a market research firm."

The next paragraph offers your talents to the company for a position related to the work mentioned in the first paragraph. This is followed by a listing of two to four similar experiences, all of which should relate to the type of position you are seeking. Finally, the last paragraph solicits the company's interest and seeks an interview.

The beauty of this unique approach is that it allows you great freedom to individualize the sales letter to the anticipated needs of the company. It can be used in place of the cover letter and resume in direct mail programs described in Chapter 19. You can't, however, eliminate the resume entirely, as you will undoubtedly be asked for it at the subsequent interview.

Further out on the unique scale is an audiocassette tape or videotape of your resume. The tape could be a rehash of the resume, it can expand on it with new information, or it can embellish existing information. Needless to say, this approach should be carefully considered, not only because it is inappropriate for many positions, but if it is not done well (professionally), it could cause your resume to be rejected when you might otherwise be qualified. Cassette tapes are inexpensive and can be used extensively; videotapes are challenging to use and expensive, and that tends to limit their use.

One young man I know was applying for a creative position with advertising agencies. Because he realized his competition would be tough, he decided on an audiotape resume. He used the theme of a boxing match, which began with an introduction of the fighters. One fighter, the applicant, was introduced with glowing credentials—relevant to the job requirements; the other fighter received no comments. The tape was completed with background music, a fight bell, and crowd noises. Several people played various roles, and upon completion, fifty tapes were made. Several job interviews were received. If this young man had used an audiotape resume for an engineering job, it would likely have received far less attention.

If you use your imagination, you will think of other unique approaches to obtaining job interviews. Although unique approaches are high risk, they are not desperate undertakings. You should not look at unique approaches as your last gasp, but instead as an effort to enhance your application procedure. Properly used with careful consideration, a unique resume or creative approach may improve your chance of obtaining great job interviews.

PART THREE

MARKETING YOURSELF

16. Introduction

Once again, repeat after me the first principle of the student interview-seeker: "Get great job interviews—it's the only way to get great jobs." And, as you know, this book is totally devoted to methods and strategies for getting you those great job interviews.

You will recall that the first step in the process is selecting those background ingredients that would most appeal to companies that have the best jobs available. If you had begun your interview-seeking preparation when you first walked into your college dorm room, you would have an outstanding resume today. Couple that resume with an effective cover letter and you should have many exciting and promising interviews.

An appealing background is a great start but it is not enough. Before beginning the pursuit of great job interviews, you now know you must complete several preparatory steps. Of these, writing the resume and constructing the cover letter are, of course, mandatory before soliciting interviews. Making good use of your university's career center is also vital. Finally, and perhaps most importantly, you need to know what you want to do and where you want to do it. All of these steps must be concluded before you venture into the world of employment interviewing.

Job Prospecting Methods

Networking
Career Centers
Direct Prospecting
Other Avenues

With your background selected and your preparation completed, it is time to let the world know who you are. This is accomplished in the third step of the interview-seeking process. I call this step personal marketing, and it is as challenging as all the previous activities combined. As the name implies, this step is simply a method of marketing yourself and your assets to achieve the ultimate goal of obtaining a good job through top job interviews.

In the following four chapters, we will explore a number of ways to prospect for jobs, including the three major ones—networking, career centers, and direct prospecting. A discussion of the rapidly growing use of the computer for interview-seeking is also included. We will set up a marketing plan for each one—an absolute necessity—and guide you from the preliminary steps to your goal of getting many great job interviews.

When Do You Start?

When do you begin your personal marketing campaign? Preparation for the job search should be completed by the end of the first semester of your senior year. This will give you the full second semester to seek interviews. While not everyone can do this as described, it is the best approach and fits in well with companies that expect to hire entry-level people at about graduation time. If you delay your job search until after graduation, many of the good positions will be filled. If you start too soon, many employers will want to see more applicants before making their choice. So begin actively marketing yourself in the second semester of your senior year.

Even though you may be a geology major seeking a position in the energy industry, the skills you will use to secure a job are selling skills. Selling is used throughout your career, but is never more critical than in the interview-seeking phase.

Thus it is important that you understand the need to utilize effective selling and prospecting strategies to obtain great interviews. What follows is not a textbook on marketing, but proven interview-getting strategies. Let's start by defining the word "prospecting." It is the activity of unearthing, pursuing, and reaching qualified candidates to sell to—in other words, reaching legitimate employers to sell your abilities to. Once you have identified prospective employers, your next step is to secure an appointment to sell to them.

As you read on, you might be tempted to select only one job-seeking approach—the one you are most comfortable with—as your total program of prospecting and selling. It is important to understand that in a good job search, you must utilize all of the approaches available to get the top interviews.

> *If you use all possible prospecting methods,*
> *you will get more interviews.*

Refer to the Senior Year Timetable—Spring Semester (on the next page) for a guide to the timing of your various personal marketing activities. As with the Senior Year Timetable—Fall Semester (see Table 9.1 on page 36), specific scheduling can be altered to meet the program of your school.

Table 16.1   SENIOR YEAR TIMETABLE—Spring Semester

Date	Activities
January	Begin to organize your networking program by identifying prospective network heads. Begin to develop a list of companies you want to pursue—complete with names of hiring authority people, addresses, and so on.
Spring Semester	Participate fully in your career center's interviewing program.
February	Send out cover letters and resumes to companies targeted in January. Spread your mailings over the month so as to make your follow-up activities efficient and manageable. Activate the network programs you developed in January. Begin to participate in your career center's interview program.
March	By this time, you should be in the midst of your direct mail prospecting follow-up activities. You should be actively involved in on-campus interviews arranged by your career center. And, you should be in the middle of your networking programs.
April/May	Focus your energies on those prospects you believe most represent opportunities to your liking. Maintain your other prospects as fall-back possibilities if your primary choices do not bear fruit. Conclude negotiations with selected firm and set starting date, job function, and compensation. Upon accepting a position, formally conclude your discussions with other firms and notify all current members of your various networks of your new position. All should be done by thank you letter.

There is a saying in the business world that is equally true in the job search: "The harder you work, the luckier you get." If you are busy looking for job interviews by networking, career center interviews, and direct prospecting, your chances of getting a great job are far better than if you use just one of these methods. The more active you are and the more approaches you use, the better your results will be.

17. Networking

As I have indicated, there are three basic approaches to securing great job interviews—networking, career centers, and direct prospecting. Because networking is the one that can be employed earliest, let's review it first.

What is networking? What does it mean? How does it work? All fair questions. Networking is a series of personal contacts leading to additional contacts. It begins with people you already know, then expands to include people who are strangers to you but known to your friends. It often goes further, from stranger to additional stranger. Networking always has a goal—for the student, the goal is to get job interviews. Sometimes networking pays off; sometimes it doesn't.

If I have heard it once, I have heard it a hundred times: "My friend got me an interview with her company." "I learned about the opening from my neighbor." "My accounting professor suggested I look into this company." These, and many other experiences, are examples of getting interviews through networks.

You can define networking as simply one person asking another person for help. A doctor's network includes patients of his who recommend him to friends looking for a new physician. A student may ask a schoolmate what good movies she's seen recently. While not related to the interview hunt, these examples illustrate networking.

> *Effective networking is work*
> *but it can be very productive work.*

The first step in beginning a network is to set up a card file containing names and pertinent information on people (usually business and other influential people) with whom you have frequent contact. You could have begun this function as early as your freshman year. The next step would be to nurture these contacts through occasional meetings and by staying in touch with them. Then, as you approach the interview-seeking stage, your contacts are in place, ready to help. If you can, you should begin developing your networks before the job search begins. However, if you didn't start it earlier, you can activate this approach in the second semester of your senior year. Once networking begins, it should continue until, and even after, you've reached your goal. In fact, after you've landed a job, you should be in touch with all your networking contacts to tell them what your new position is and to thank them for their help.

Each student can have several networks. Every person you know represents a potential network beginning. If you know ten people, each one can serve as the start of a network. Thus, it is possible to have ten networks working simultaneously. In fact, the more networks you have, the better.

Who Do You Ask?

Who can you ask for help in building your networks?

1. Relatives—of course. They would certainly be anxious to help you.
2. College people—professors, deans, advisors, to name a few.
3. Friends of your parents—they can produce networks that can spread throughout the country.
4. Leaders in your organizations—from the church, usually the clergy, coaches of athletic teams, leaders of college organizations, heads of groups you participate in.
5. Businesspeople you have met along the way—you should have solidified these contacts as they were made, even if they preceded your use of networking.
6. Members of your peer group who already have jobs—they may know of openings at their firm.
7. Associates at companies you have worked at previously—past employers, coworkers.
8. Alumni of your college—they represent excellent networking possibilities. Your university's alumni office has an alumni directory you can use, or your career center may offer an alumni contact program.

This undertaking—creating a list of potential networking leaders—should produce a large number of people to start your networks. Each network can represent from one to five contacts. If your list of possible networks numbers ten, for example, you have the potential of talking with and perhaps getting interviews for jobs from a group of up to fifty people. That's what I call a darn good start.

The Ideal Network

Let's examine an ideal network. Your first network should start with your parents. Of course, these people know you well and can be expected to spend considerable energy promoting "their" network. Suppose you have ambitions to be an engineer. Your parents may or may not have engineering expertise, but if they don't, they probably know someone who does. The first step in this network is for your parents to ask their engineering friends if they would spend some time with you discussing the engineering field.

After your parents have set up a meeting for you with one of their engineering friends, take a list of written questions to the meeting and refer to it during your conversation. Often, it takes only one or two solid questions to get the session going, after which it will flow smoothly. You should also plan on taking notes during the meeting.

Your goals with each segment of the network are to:

1. Impress each individual with your maturity and interest in the field. To do this, you must prepare for the meeting and try to control its direction.
2. Learn as much as you can about your industry of preference from the meeting.
3. Determine if the contact has a position for which you could interview. Often the best way to get that information is to ask an outright question, "Mr. Smith, does your company have any openings for which I might be an appropriate candidate?"
4. Secure an additional leg of the network. No matter how the meeting goes (even if you get a job interview), it should always end by asking, "Mr. Smith, do you know anyone else I could talk with about engineering?" You may get more referrals than you expect.

After you have impressed the individual with your maturity and interest and have had all your questions answered; after you have determined whether there is a position available currently; and after you have acquired additional names for your network—then it is time to move on. Regardless of the meeting's outcome, it is important to send a thank you note (which can be handwritten, if done legibly) to the individual you met with. You should also leave your resume with the person or send it with your thank you note. If the individual has arranged an appointment or made a referral for you, a thank you phone call after you've met with the new contact is required. That phone call gives you another opportunity to talk with the previous network contact, who might have thought of some additional ways to help. Repeat these steps throughout all segments of all networks.

Sooner or later, a network will come to a halt either because you terminate it (once you have landed a job) or because it runs out of connecting contacts. No network goes on forever.

Networking succeeds best when appointments are arranged to discuss a specific industry. They rarely succeed if you try to set up a meeting by asking if there is a position for which you could interview. With this direct approach, the answer is generally yes or no, and the yeses are rare. With a no, you lose the opportunity to talk with a knowledgeable individual who might be able to refer you to another, more likely, person. The network expands best when each individual in it is asked to discuss their specific industry, not whether there is a job opening.

After the parent's network is under way, what's the best one to set up next? It is usually a network of people who are in the industry you are pursuing. In this case, it begins with the engineers you know. Ask them for the opportunity to discuss the industry. Handle this network in the same manner as the one established by your parents.

Follow that network by reviewing the list of all the other adults you know. The list can be long (as you saw above) but that's all to the better. Most on the list will not be fluent about engineering, but many of them will know someone who is. Begin these networks with a personal phone call. Ask your contacts if they know someone with engineering expertise. If they say yes, ask if they would make an introductory call to facilitate a meeting. If they are unwilling to do so, ask if it would be permissible to use their name when you make the call to set up the meeting. Without a personal connection, a network contact is difficult to arrange.

Recordkeeping

Because each network has a life of its own and a unique direction, and because you will have many networks working simultaneously, it is important to keep accurate, up-to-date records on all of your network contacts. Use a journal or notecard system to ensure that you take the appropriate steps and record results along the way.

When a university asks its graduating seniors how they got their first job, many of them will say through a friend or a contact they knew. What they are really saying is that they got their job through networking. Often, the best-qualified applicant doesn't get a job that ultimately is secured by a less-qualified person because the former individual didn't have the right contacts. Networking will give you many contacts.

18. Career Centers Revisited

We have already spent some time discussing the assets a university's career center can offer your job-seeking effort. But career centers are really two organizations—one that assists you in preparing for the job search, the other that arranges job interviews for you with interested corporations. These interviews are generally held on campus and often produce surprising results.

Some students are unenthusiastic about interviews with corporations arranged by their career centers. I'm not sure why, but perhaps one reason is that students think this approach doesn't work. They see interviews taking place but rarely hear of anyone who actually gets a job through on-campus interviewing. The idea that corporations are looking for just a few new employees and yet hold hundreds of interviews at many schools can be discouraging.

> *Utilize your career center to*
> *get as many job interviews as possible.*

Yet you must understand that getting a job is often accomplished through the "numbers game." If you have twenty interviews, your chance of getting a job is X, but if you have forty interviews, your chances double to 2X. Thus the more interviews you have, the sooner your talents and desires will be matched with the needs of a company. And there is no easier way of getting interviews than through career center sponsorship. Incidentally, my first job out of college came from an interview that was arranged by my university's career center. It can be done.

Common Traits

How is it accomplished? The career center interviewing program at each school differs, but they all have a few things in common. In general, each career center arranges for corporations to come to their school

117

for campus interviews, and each center sets up students to meet them. From this point, the process varies. Some colleges require that students complete a preparation program before they are allowed to sign up for interviews. This is done to ensure that students have some knowledge of the interviewing process, and to provide the student with job-seeking information and interviewing techniques. Some schools don't require that step, others require more. Ask your career center what its requirements are.

Perhaps the area where schools differ most widely is in the process of selecting which students get to interview with which companies. Regardless of the method used, there is always the question of whether it is being done fairly. The truth is, there is probably no way the process can be completely fair to everyone. If you think about it, this is simply a reflection on life itself. Things just can't be equal for all. Nonetheless, the system, flawed though it may be, works, and a student who plays by the rules will have a fair shot.

Generally, colleges post in some conspicuous location the names of each corporation sending representatives for campus interviewing. This posting usually includes the type of position the interview is for, the time and place it is to be held, and any other information required for the interview. One of the more prevalent additional items is the type of student the company wants to interview. For example, if the company is in the oil business and is looking for budding geologists, they will not want to interview English majors. Although this may seem to reduce an English major's opportunities, it is in fact a fair process because it allows more geology majors to interview for positions for which they already have preliminary credentials and interest.

Selection Process

Thus, the most controversial aspect of on-campus interviews is the process of who gets selected to interview with which company. The conflict arises because there are often more students interested in interviews than there are interview time slots. For example, if a company agrees to hold interviews at your school for two days with fourteen interview slots each day, there will be only twenty-eight students who can interview with that company. Yet, sixty students may want interviews. Some of them will be disappointed. How are the lucky ones selected?

The system varies from school to school. The least complex but the most chaotic is simply the old "first come, first served" method. Once the job interview is posted, you can sign up without precondition. The early bird gets the worm, but, unfortunately, it isn't always possible to be an early bird. After all, some students have to attend classes. This approach could allow a handful of students to have a disproportionately large number of interviews, and others very few. Nonetheless, some schools use this method.

Another frequently employed approach is a system of bidding for specific job interviews. This method also varies from school to school, but it does permit a fairer distribution of job interviews. One school I know of uses the following process:

First the college assigns corporate interviewing sessions to a ten-week period in the fall and another ten-week period in the spring. The fall program is geared to students graduating in December. Each student who completes the preinterview program required by the university is given 500 points for each week of interviews. When an interview is posted, students "bid" for the interview with some of their weekly points. The maximum bid per interview is 250. A 250-point bid says, "I really want this interview," while a 100-point bid says, "I'd like the interview, but won't lose any sleep if I don't get it."

Students selected for an interview will be those who bid the most points. Those not accepted for an interview lose the points they bid. If, for example, there are 28 interview opportunities and 28 students who bid 250 points, all 28 will get interviews, but any student who bid less than 250 points would not. If more than 28 people bid 250 points, then it could come down to first come, first served among those who bid 250 points. Other schools might draw 28 names from a hat. If fewer than 28 students bid 250 points, the top 28 bidders get the appointments and that could include students who bid down to 100 points or less.

With this method, students are not guaranteed an interview even if they bid the maximum number of points. Practically speaking though, students who participate in this program get interviews.

Another method is to divide students by interests (marketing people in this group, engineers in that group) and rotate each group through related job interviews. If 480 interview slots are to be available with accounting firms in the spring session and 240 accounting students want interviews, each student would receive two interviews. The selection of the companies for those interviews could be done on a purely random, rotating basis.

In some cases, interviews are arranged only after the interviewing company has received and reviewed the resumes of students seeking interviews with them. The employer "weeds out" applicants they are not

.sed solely on the resume's ingredients. Thus, the student .e interview has already passed the first checkpoint—a positive . to a resume, further supporting our earlier contention that the .me is the key selling document for the student. Those whose resumes fall short proceed no further with that company. Of course, students who don't get on-campus interviews with a desired company may still pursue that firm directly using the techniques described in the next chapter.

Supply and Demand

Regardless of the system used, it comes down to the old story of supply and demand. There is a finite supply of job interviews offered and frequently a larger demand from students. If there is broad interest among participating students, there will be fewer interviews per student. Conversely, if student interest is low, there will be no problem getting interviews.

It is at this point that you have to concentrate. In the point method described earlier, you have to make careful judgments to avoid squandering your 500 weekly points. If you bid 250 points twice in a week to secure interviews with popular employers and come up empty-handed, you will have thrown away one tenth of your career center's interviewing points. This will also occur if you bid 100 points for five interviews and get none of them because they were popular with the overall student group.

To succeed, you have to make some sound judgments on how to manage your bidding points. It's fair to say that marketing students historically flock to marketing-oriented companies like Frito Lay, Procter & Gamble, and RJR Nabisco. You can be sure their interviews will be "sold out"—all interview slots will be filled, and if they are allocated by a point system, only a maximum bid will have a chance of being selected. If, however, a company looking for marketing people comes to campus without a strong marketing reputation, it is possible that a 100-point bid will get the nod.

The judgment call here is how popular you believe the company posted for interviews will be. If it is popular, your strategy is either a maximum bid (always with the risk of failure and loss of points) or no bid at all. Perhaps you would be wiser to bid 125 points for four less-popular companies and hope to get them all (or at least some of them).

Doing Your Homework

If I were to be a spring semester graduate, I would spend a lot of time in the career center during the *fall* semester learning how the interview procedure plays out. You can call this "fall training" if you'd like. See how the process works, find out how the bidding process unfolds and what strategies seem to succeed. You will be far better prepared than your competition for the "regular season" in the spring.

The other strategic approach that makes great sense to me is working with the career center counselors. These people know how the system works, can, on occasion, give you a helping hand, and are not immune to a good sales effort by you. Career center counselors are human and respond, as we all do, to good approaches. Before the "regular season," make friends with these influential people—ask for help, show sincerity, exhibit enthusiasm, be attentive, be visible, be nice. I'm not saying you're going to get any special favors, but I'm not saying you won't either. Start the process of selling yourself to your career center counselors early—good things can come of it.

Getting Interviewing Experience

Everybody agrees that people applying for jobs do better in their interviews if they have had interviewing experience. Rarely do your first interviews shine. The dilemma, of course, is that most students don't have much interviewing experience. They learn interviewing techniques during important on-campus interviews—on-the-job training, so to speak. Consequently, students often interview poorly during these initial sessions.

How do we get around this problem? There are three obvious methods of gaining interviewing experience. The first is to read a good book on the subject. From this, you will learn some of the techniques, but you will have no opportunity to practice them. The second approach, far more beneficial, is to participate in on-campus mock interviews organized by many career centers. This is a great opportunity to learn and practice good interviewing skills. Many schools, as mentioned earlier, videotape these mock interviews, and the benefits to you can be significant.

The third approach to gaining interviewing experience is one that career center people won't like. Even if you're not interested in a particular company's on-campus interview, sign up for it if you have points available and hope you get it. It will provide you with a great chance to learn interviewing skills and practice techniques. There are two reasons why career centers don't like the idea of an uninterested student taking interview time from an interested student. It does a disservice to the corporation, which expects to interview students who have a sincere interest and, of course, it can deny an interested student a key interview. Recognizing the concerns voiced here and that learning ethics early in

` is important (but also recognizing the need to sharp-
.ving skills), try to select those companies that will not
..e amount of interest from students. Those are usually com-
.at can be selected for an interview by students using just a 100-
.. bid. Who knows, you might even find a great job from it.

The career center can be enormously helpful in arranging interviews for you with corporations looking for entry-level people for specific job opportunities. Many students don't participate in the career center's on-campus interviewing program, and that's great for those who do. As a result, there are more job interviews available for a smaller number of interested students. One of them should be you.

19. Direct Prospecting

As stated previously, graduating seniors seeking interviews with the best companies should use all proven methods to obtain those interviews. Networking can be very rewarding, and interviews arranged by your career center equally so. But direct prospecting is the one method that produces the greatest number of interviews for students year-in and year-out. By prospecting we mean making a direct, personal approach to specific, targeted companies.

As you might suspect, this method is not glamorous, exciting, or easy. Networking and career center interviews are created at least partially (often significantly) from efforts made by others. True, the student has a role to play in producing the interview, but that role is frequently secondary. To successfully prospect for interviews, you must be proactive from beginning to end. No one will be handling any of the load for you. You must begin the program, carry it out, and bring it to a successful conclusion, all without help. While this method is the most successful of the interview-seeking approaches, it is also the most work and the most frustrating. But it does work!

Via the Post Office

There are two ways to prospect for interviews. The first is via direct mail, the second utilizes the personal approach. Let's discuss the direct mail process first.

The majority of employment inquiries are by mail. You send a cover letter and resume to a key individual at a selected corporation, and all subsequent activities revolve around that key person. Let's start by listing the procedural steps required to properly utilize direct mail. We will discuss each step in more detail later in the chapter.

Direct Mail Steps

1. **Compile a list of companies in your desired field and in your preferred geographical location to pursue for interviews.**
2. **Identify the key individuals to contact for an interview.**
3. **Send your cover letter and resume to that person.**
4. **Follow every mailing with a call (or calls, if necessary).**

The first item to address in prospecting for interviews is really a very important issue: How do you determine which companies to pursue? There are so many and they are all different. We will assume that you know what business you want to be in and where geographically you want your job to be located, because you cannot effectively prospect for interviews until those two ingredients are decided. When you make the decision on what business and which location you want, your choices of target companies narrow to a workable number.

Let's say that you are seeking a position as a commercial loan associate. In this case, the obvious companies to approach are banks. There are other companies in the commercial loan business, but banks are the logical ones. As it turns out, locating banks is easy—they are all listed in the Yellow Pages of the city telephone directory.

Yellow Pages et al.

So we have quickly discovered a prime listing of companies—the telephone directory. While this approach isn't very scientific, in many cases, it is a good start. But where do you turn when the telephone directory isn't satisfactory? There are several sources:

1. Generally, every industry has a trade association. These associations always have a listing of members—often in directory form. To find the name of a specific industry's trade association, call one of the companies in the industry, ask for the office of the president, and request the name and phone number of their trade association. Then call the association and have them send you a list of their members. Usually, the list will include addresses and phone numbers.
2. Virtually every city has a chamber of commerce. It is amazing how much information chambers of commerce have about businesses in their area. Among all the data available, chambers of commerce can provide you with a list of companies in their market area and offer considerable additional information, if desired. The chamber staff is well equipped to answer your questions and able to provide detailed information on local business activity.
3. Many college career centers also have listings of companies, often

broken down by types of businesses. While you are benefiting from all the assets your career center provides, check out their directories of corporations. These may even include the names of key people to contact. Career centers also have access to companies via multiple computer programs.

4. If you know what industry you prefer but don't care where you locate, investment brokerage firms have a wide assortment of information on publicly held companies. This information is generally housed in their home office research department but can often be accessed through branch sales offices. While investment firms aren't in business to assist strangers in their job search, they will make investment publications and services available to you. It will help, though, to go through someone you know who works at a brokerage company.

5. Your local library is absolutely loaded with materials to help you identify companies to pursue. Libraries house a wide assortment of directories, many of which can assist you in selecting appropriate targets. Ask the librarian for help and use the now-prevalent library computer system.

6. Periodically, through networks you have established, a number of appropriate companies' names will surface, and they should be added to your list of possible targets.

7. Finally, of course, you may know people who actually work in the industry in which you have an interest. They should be among your first contacts, because in addition to being able to provide you with the names of other companies in the industry, they may even be able to advise you of job openings at their own companies (networking). If there is an opening in their company in your area of interest, your friend can get you to the right interviewing person promptly and without fuss. In fact, many companies tend to hire people referred to them by their employees rather than strangers off the street. The rationale is that employees would be unlikely to refer new employees who don't measure up to company standards.

After you have gone through all of the sources mentioned above, you should have a long list of companies to pursue. While you should apply to every company you identify in your selected business field, one guideline might be helpful: Companies that are most likely to be hiring are those that are growing the fastest. These companies usually have more need for "new blood" than do slower-growing or stagnant companies. You can't rule out any corporation, but your best opportunities may come from those on a faster track.

Because in the course of your job search you will be pursuing many companies, you will be wise to create a card file system (or a reasonable alternative) containing a separate card for each company. This will be similar to the card system you created for your networking program. In this system, record all your contacts with each company, with particular reference to specific individuals, and a chronological listing of dates and events that have transpired with the company. After a while, it becomes difficult to remember what you have done with each company, to whom you have spoken and when, and what the next step should be. Without careful recordkeeping, you might miss important dates and important stages, and that will work against you as you move through the interviewing process.

Who Has the Authority?

The next step in direct mail prospecting is to identify the right person to receive your cover letter and resume. That right person is the individual who has the authority to hire—the difficulty comes in determining who that is.

> *Direct your prospecting approach to the individual who has the authority to hire.*

First, let's address this issue by stating that you should avoid applying to corporate personnel departments, often called human resources departments. While these departments serve many useful purposes, they almost never have hiring authority. They perform a "screening" function—the first step in the interviewing process. Their purpose is to refer qualified candidates to the hiring authority, and they do that by weeding out individuals with apparent background inadequacies. Your best bet is to "go over their head" with a direct approach to the individual who has the hiring authority.

Why bypass the personnel department? For good reason—hiring is a highly personalized decision. People hire people they like or relate well to (provided, of course, that the individual has the basic qualifications for the position). Also, people often interpret stated job requirements differently. There are many cases where a hirer has employed an individual whom the personnel department would have screened out. Why give the company two opportunities to reject you—go right to the top!

The worst thing that could happen if you go directly to the individual with the hiring authority is a referral back to the personnel department for screening. However, that's better than going to personnel initially since they will probably review a candidate more carefully if the hiring authority referred the candidate to them than if the applicant came directly to them through the mail.

Generally, the individual with hiring authority is in charge of the department of the company you are interested in. In that connection, let's continue our example of the student who wants to become a commercial loan associate. The best approach for this student is to find out who is in charge of the commercial loan department in each of the targeted banks. In this example, we do not know who the head of the department is, but solving that problem should be easy. Simply call the bank and ask for the name of the head of the commercial loan department. Make sure you get the complete name and double check the spelling and address with the telephone operator. You now have the name of the person to whom you should apply. If you can't find out that person's name, address your cover letter by title to the head of the department in which you would like to work, such as Manager, Commercial Loan Department.

While the head of the appropriate department usually knows its needs, and is often the one with the authority to hire, there may be times when she is not the right person. But if you have written to her, don't worry—an application sent to the department head (even if that is not the correct individual) will usually find its way to the appropriate person.

We now have reached our second goal—to whom to apply. A related goal—determining if there is a position open—is the next step. When department heads receive your application, several things can happen: They can refer it for review to the appropriate hiring authority if they are not it; they can review it, reject it, and file it without a response (or they can send you a rejection letter); or, on a more positive note, they can review it and invite you in for an interview. This will only be done if they like what they see on the resume and only if there is a position available.

Ignore No Prospect

Now that we have determined the correct people to apply to, we need to decide how many companies to approach. The answer is simple—all of them! While you undoubtedly will have some initial preferences among companies in your universe, applying to all of them gives you much greater flexibility and an excellent opportunity to make intelligent comparisons. The more exposure you have to the breadth of the industry, the better able you will be to evaluate the alternatives. You might even find a wonderful employment opportunity at one of your initially less-favored companies.

So, off go your letters and resumes. After they are mailed, prepare for frustration because you will have no idea what kind of response you will get or, for that matter, whether you will get any response at all. And, unfortunately, employers rarely consider applications as quickly as you would like them to.

Hence the need for the last mandatory step after sending the resumes—your follow-up procedure. This usually takes the form of a phone call to the individual to whom the letter was addressed. Your chances of getting an interview increase dramatically if you make your follow-up calls and decrease measurably if you don't.

The follow-up call also gives you the opportunity to back your written sales pitch with some verbal selling. Finally, individuals find it more difficult to say no to someone in person than in writing.

Tuesday, Tuesday, Tuesday

Let's talk a minute about the timing of the follow-up call. There are two elements to the timing question—when do you want the resume to arrive and when do you plan to make the follow-up call? In most cases, an application should not arrive on a Monday. Businesspeople have a week's worth of work ahead of them on Monday, and it can be a very busy day. (If you were seeking an interview with me, don't have your letter arrive on Monday. I have too many things to do on Monday, and your resume is not likely to be one of them.) Friday is usually undesirable as well because of the ease with which your letter can be forgotten over the weekend and further lost in the press of Monday's business. That leaves Tuesday, Wednesday, and Thursday as appropriate letter-arrival times.

Before we decide which of those days are best for the letter to be received, we need to address the timing of your follow-up call. Don't make your call on the day the letter is likely to be received. It may not have arrived or, if it has, the individual to whom you have written might not have had an opportunity to read it yet. The day after receipt is not good either for the same reasons. Ideally, follow up your letter with a call on the second or third day after it has been received. If your follow-up call comes much later than the third day, you run the risk of your application being forgotten. Another timing question: Do you want to make the follow-up call after a weekend has passed? The answer to that is no—too many things could supersede your application over the weekend.

So, in conclusion, your best bet is to have your resume arrive on Tuesday so that you can begin your follow-up calls on Thursday. If you can't get through on Thursday, you still have Friday to call again without suffering weekend interference. To have a letter arrive at a local company on Tuesday, it should be mailed the prior Friday. It will be there by

Tuesday for sure, but even if it arrives on Monday, a follow-up call on Thursday will still be satisfactory.

Once again, here are the chronological steps for mailing the resume:

1. Resume mailed: Friday
2. Resume received: Monday/Tuesday
3. Resume followed up: Thursday/Friday

The Barrier

Unfortunately, the follow-up call is a complex and frustrating requirement because getting through to hirers means getting past their secretaries—rarely an easy task. Secretaries screen calls and can prevent you from gaining access to their boss. "Pleasantly persistent" is the guideline in this situation. If you persist, you will in most cases get through to the individual to whom you sent the letter. If the boss is out, call again. Ask the secretary when the best time to call would be. Call several times, and if you still have no response, leave your name for a callback. If that doesn't occur in a few days, call again. Ultimately, you might need to send the hiring authority a second letter politely asking for a response. Every job applicant has a right to a response! While some employers make a habit of not responding, it is downright rude and inconsiderate. If you are being handled in that fashion, you have the right to persist and nothing to lose if you do.

In my work with college students seeking their first employment, I have become acutely aware of how much effort is required to make contact with the individual to whom they wrote. After a while it becomes a game with them—at what time should we call today? Follow-up calls are made daily, and periodically they leave their name for a callback—often to no avail but with frequent enough success to warrant the effort.

Despite the disappointment of not being able to reach employers easily, follow-up calls must be made and repeated regularly until contact is made. Keep in mind that if you are applying to individuals who have hiring authority, they usually have a full-time job and the hiring portion is a small, occasional part of it. In many cases, it is not that hirers are trying to avoid you—they are often very busy, out of town, in a meeting, or performing other functions. You simply need to keep trying.

So, in prospecting for interviews by direct mail, identify target companies, determine the individuals with hiring authority, send your cover letter and resume to them, and follow up with phone calls. The process works.

Incidentally, there is a growing trend for students to fax, rather than mail, their cover letter and resume to target companies. This method is used to speed up the application process and "grab" some attention. As always, it is imperative that you follow up your faxed application two days later with a phone call to get an appointment. As is my custom, I respond to all faxed resumes I receive.

Knocking on Doors

Prospecting for interviews in person involves much the same process. The in-person method simply means that you appear at a company without an appointment for an interview with the hiring authority. Beforehand, you still need to identify target companies and determine the hiring authority, but instead of sending a letter, you drop in unannounced.

In most cases, you won't get an interview on your surprise visit. You may leave, however, having arranged an appointment for a later date. And, even if you don't get an appointment, you can always leave your resume. Because this is a strong likelihood, plan ahead. Bring with you a notepad and envelope. If the best you can get by arriving without an appointment is the opportunity to leave your resume, write (neatly) a personal note to the hirer asking, among other comments, for an interview, and put both the note and the resume in the envelope. Then write the hirer's name on the envelope and seal it. The odds are very high that the interviewer will get your resume and read it. Follow-up phone calls are still mandatory if you want to get an appointment. Of course, it is entirely possible you will be granted an interview while you are there.

As you can see, there are three possible gains that can result from an in-person call on a company:

1. An interview
2. An appointment for a later interview
3. An opportunity to leave a resume

At the least, you could learn if the company has positions available that fit your skills. In some cases, particularly in small companies, receptionists know what positions the firm has open. You might be asked by the receptionist, for instance, what your job objective is. They can often tell you whether the company is seeking applicants for that specialization. In these situations, it's better to give a broad objective so as not to be prematurely excluded by a clerical employee who thought your very specific job preference wouldn't fit the company's needs.

In this chapter, I have devoted much more space to direct prospecting for interviews by mail than by the in-person method. You should not be misled into thinking I favor one approach over the other simply because one takes more space to describe than the other. Both methods are equally important, and, in fact, the in-person approach is usually more effective, though it takes considerably more time.

Follow These Rules

Here are some additional rules to follow. *First*, every interview with a company—first through last, successful or not—should be followed up with a thank you note or a personal call. The letter need not be long or necessarily typed (if your handwriting is legible).

Second, never assume a negative. This is a favorite guideline of mine. In the case of direct prospecting for interviews, this means you never assume a company has no interest in you. It's easy to avoid pursuing a possibility if you think they will have no interest in you or if you think they have no available positions. If persistently pursued, many of those situations turn out favorably. Don't take no for an answer, never assume they're not interested, and don't further assume they have no appropriate openings. Start out believing every company has openings and is eager to interview you—invoke the power of positive thinking.

Third, when sending an application to an appropriate department head, send a copy with a resume to the head of that firm's personnel department as well. This might produce an interest in a related position elsewhere in the company that the department head wouldn't know of.

Fourth, if you are unable to determine who has the hiring authority at a specific company, you may write to that firm's personnel department. You will still need to make your follow-up calls, but to the addressee in the personnel department.

Last, when you have secured an interview, you would be wise to do as much homework on the company as you can. Before the interview, ask them to send you their annual report or some public relations material. Call the firm's stockholder relations department if the company is publicly held or the office of the president if it is not. These people are used to providing this information. Also, go to the library and ask for help on how you can learn more about a particular company and industry. They can usually be of great assistance. There are other sources of information, but these should give you a good starting point.

20. The Other Possibilities

Experience tells us that some 90 percent of the jobs obtained by college graduates come from the efforts they make using the three main interview-seeking strategies—networking, utilization of career center interviewing programs, and direct prospecting for interviews. For that reason most, if not all, of your interviewing activities should be devoted to these approaches.

> *Aside from the big three, there are*
> *many other ways to prospect for interviews.*

But there are several other avenues available to you that can supplement the core efforts described in the three previous chapters. There are two reasons why you should use them.

Prospecting, whether for interviews or in selling, succeeds best when every prospecting approach is used. It is simply not sufficient, for example, to use networking as your only method of seeking out great interviews. Nor is it enough in the competitive environment you face to use just the combination of networking and career center opportunities. It is essential to include direct prospecting for interviews in conjunction with networking and career centers. But in order to cover the broadest spectrum of job possibilities, your efforts should include the additional approaches described below. The more exposure you have, the more opportunities you can uncover. It's true in selling and it's true in seeking interviews.

The second reason to use additional prospecting methods is that you may uncover viable alternatives to the companies you are pursuing. For instance, if you want to be a salesperson, you may be pleasantly surprised to learn that virtually every industry and every company has a sales force. That includes the heavy hitters (General Motors, AT&T, IBM, and so on) as well as small, local companies. As a budding salesperson, if your focus is on just one specific industry, you will not be exposed to the enormous variety of selling positions available throughout all business. Also, while direct selling is an honorable profession, related work (such as marketing, advertising, customer service) can be equally challenging, and if you are a qualified sales candidate, you could measure up well for those positions as well.

In summary, utilize all available interview-seeking methods. That will lead to a greater number of job interviews and a greater exposure to related positions.

What are these additional interview-seeking activities?

1. Computer services
2. Newspaper employment sections
3. Employment agencies
4. Job fairs

The Omnipotent Computer

Perhaps the fastest growing job prospecting method is the use of the computer. In fact, five years ago, it was a nonevent; now it is rivaling the core prospecting methods discussed previously. And a student need not be a computer expert, or even have a computer, to access computer job information since it is easy to do and your career center will find a computer for you to use.

The good news is that computer job searching is exploding; the bad news is that there are scores of programs and they are changing rapidly. Described below are some that were current when this book was written but may be different or obsolete three years from now. The state-of-the-art computer job search function is moving at lightning speed, and your best bet is to work with your college's career center and take their advice on the best services to use.

What follows are examples of programs available today. While they may change over time, the descriptions will give you an idea of what you can expect in computer-driven job prospecting. For example, JOB-TRAK is a relatively mature Internet service having been established in the late 1980s. JOBTRAK is used by a large number of college career centers to help manage their job-listing services. In fact, there are over 100,000 employers across the nation that have placed full- or part-time job openings on this network. JOBTRAK has developed Jobs On-Line and Employers On-Line, which provide job listings targeted specifically to college students. Their listings can be instantaneously altered as needed by the companies as their circumstances change.

Also exploding is the computer-oriented E-mail system of searching out good job prospects. E-mail is also going through significant changes, so once again specific services may be here today but gone tomorrow.

Currently, E-mail is used primarily as a method for employer and prospective employee to communicate with each other. But the outlook is for more extensive use of E-mail. For example, for those major corporations offering many job openings, applicants can use E-mail to send in their resume. The resume would then "hook up" with an employer's job computers, which search incoming resumes to find matches with existing job availabilities. Interviews could result from these connections.

Decisive Quest is a currently active computer software program that eliminates the need for a resume in the early going. The program leads you through a "fill-in-the-blanks" college template that records your background and experiences. This information is then uploaded to Decisive Quest's national database. When your data are matched with a company's hiring needs, an interview can be created.

Even further along in the computer job search explosion are programs developed by specific corporations that enhance their ability to obtain candidates for their positions while providing a service for applicants. One that has come to my attention is Engineer Your Career offered by Texas Instruments (T.I.). This is an interactive program complete with disk that begins with a careful look at Texas Instruments today and follows with their Career Mapper and Fit Check Survey, both of which the applicant completes. The disk is then returned to T.I., which provides each applicant with an Engineer Your Career Planning Packet—a personalized profile and career map. Finally, T.I. will evaluate your electronic resume for a possible match with existing T.I. job opportunities.

An attempt has been made here to introduce you to the wide variety of job search and prospecting tools being developed through the use of the personal computer. The programs mentioned above just scratch the surface. I again caution you that it is an ever changing and rapidly expanding arena and your best bet to stay on top of developments is to consult with your college career center. They will show what computer-oriented prospecting programs are most beneficial to your needs.

The Daily Newspaper et al.

A second interview-seeking approach is a little more conventional. Every newspaper has an employment section where specific job openings are advertised to attract qualified applicants. The daily paper in your city will list opportunities in your local area. If your college is in a small-to-medium-sized town, subscribe for a few months to the daily paper of the nearest major city. If you want to work in a specific city that isn't near your school, subscribe to the paper of that town. It will arrive by mail several days late, but job openings are rarely filled quickly. In addition, companies often advertise their job availabilities in college newspapers. Make sure you are reading your school paper regularly.

For a broader picture of the national employment market, *The Wall Street Journal* is your best bet. Most jobs are advertised in Tuesday's issue, and they may be located anywhere in the country. *The Wall Street Journal* also publishes a weekly paper, the *National Business Employment Weekly*, which is devoted entirely to job openings. *The New York Times* is also often loaded with job possibilities. These openings may be for locations outside New York City as well as in the city. You will find extensive employment ads in most major city papers.

When responding to a newspaper ad, you might start your cover letter as follows:

> In the Sunday edition of the *Los Angeles Times*, you indicated an interest in applicants for a position as a commercial artist. The purpose of this letter and enclosed resume is to arrange an interview with you for that job.

One point to be aware of if you use newspapers as a source of job prospects: Most positions listed are for people with some experience. From time to time, ads will appear for an entry-level individual, but not often.

Don't overlook the use of employment agencies. Every city has several. Employment agencies do what a computer match-up service does—they put applicants and job openings together. With the agencies, it is done on a more personal basis, often coupled with sound advice and counseling. Also, they concentrate in a specific local business community as opposed to a countrywide focus. The agencies are there to aid your effort, and they often provide ongoing assistance during the interview chase.

Another avenue to great job interviews is attending job fairs. These programs are held in large and medium-sized cities and give employers the opportunity to meet with fair attendees to discuss job openings at their company. Corporations with job openings rent booths at the fair. Representatives of these companies work the booths and are available to talk with attendees about positions the company has open. For a small fee, you can attend job fairs and have the opportunity to talk with prospective employers. Take a supply of resumes along with you to give to appropriate company representatives, if requested.

The job fair is not a job interview. It is primarily a place for attendees to see what types of positions are open and find out how to pursue them. This process can lead to an interview— but in and of itself, it is not an interview.

The alert student will recognize other interview-seeking activities along the way. The most successful students use all of the interview-seeking methods described here as well as others they may discover from time to time.

21. What Happens If None of This Works?

At this point in the book, you have received a complete education in how to get great job interviews. The methods described are proven, effective, and, when followed carefully, result in excellent interviews. Properly carried out, you will be the recipient of many great job interviews and subsequent job offers.

Is it possible to follow all of the suggestions in the book and still not get interviews? Yes it is. But in 95 percent of the cases, you will have a supply of great interviews.

What do you do, though, if all of the interview search preparation and personal marketing does not produce interviews? You will be pleased to know that, if you have not had the expected success, there are several steps you can take to restore yourself to the right track. And the first step is simply to remain positive—do not get discouraged.

> *Stay positive—*
> *do not get discouraged.*

After all, no one said getting great interviews and great jobs was going to be easy. For some it's easier than others, but because the process may have been more difficult for you than someone else is no reason to be depressed. You know the old expression, "When the going gets tough, the tough get going." That could be you.

There is only one aspect of this whole program you can't change—the experience you offer to the employer. By the time you're a senior, all of that is accomplished. The rest of the interview-seeking process can be altered even to the extent of redoing your resume and/or cover letter.

The Reexamination

In addition to remaining positive, what are the other steps you can take to reaim your rifle? The first is to carefully examine the process you've been going through. Try to determine whether you've followed all the recommendations in this book wholeheartedly. Perhaps you haven't pursued each one to the letter. In your reexamination of the process, tighten up on the details. For example, maybe you've followed up on only some applications—follow up on all of them in the future.

Review Steps
1. **Examine the process you've been through.**
2. **Reexamine yourself.**
3. **Review your job goals.**
4. **Reevaluate your geographic preferences.**
5. **Improve your resume and cover letter.**
6. **Reread this book.**

Since we're in the reexamination process, do the same with yourself. Try to understand what motivates you, with an eye on making sure you have a solid direction in mind. All too often, I've seen college students seeking employment without a specific goal besides the goal of getting a good job. They don't know what they want to do or where they want to do it. To an experienced interviewer, this lack of direction is obvious and is usually sufficient to reject a candidate. Just wanting a good job is not enough when all around you there is competition, competition, competition!

One of the most obvious reexamination steps is a review of your specific job preference. Perhaps you need to sharpen up your job objective. The first question to ask then is: "Does the job I'd like to have really exist?" As novices in getting jobs, students sometimes have job fantasies—envisioning a job unrelated to the real world. Try to find out if your job preference is realistic or not. Also, determine if your job objective is too narrow. If so, you might be missing opportunities because your job goal excludes you from consideration for related positions. You can also err on the side of having a job objective that is too broad. Stating that you'd like to work in the accounting department might be too general for companies that have many types of positions within their accounting department.

If you believe your job desires are accurate and realistic, then perhaps you should expand the definition of the position. Earlier, we mentioned a student who expressed an interest in sales. Perhaps companies that interviewed him didn't feel he had sales potential. If you keep getting no's along the way, that may be a signal to expand your job preference to include positions related to sales such as marketing, account servicing, market research, and so on. By expanding your job objective, you may open up related possibilities that otherwise might be closed to you.

One of my young friends pursued a creative advertising job but got no takers. The reasons at this point are not important, but he decided to expand his job goal to include an advertising account executive position. This broadened his appeal, and he did receive an advertising job.

Geography Again

Another point to consider as you proceed through this reexamination phase is geography. Many students fall short of their job expectations because their chosen city doesn't have appropriate opportunities. For example, there are very few petroleum engineering jobs in Des Moines, Iowa. If your initial search fails to produce a job there, broaden your geographical territory. That doesn't mean you need to jump from Des Moines to the whole country, but you could expand the territory to include the Southwest market where most energy activity is located. This area includes Dallas, Houston, New Orleans, to name just the big cities, as well as many other medium-sized ones.

By broadening your territory, you will be able to include many, many more companies in your search, some of which could be looking for talented people like you. Once you have reexamined your geographical preferences, follow the steps in this book carefully. You'll be a winner.

There is another step you should take when evaluating your lack of success in getting good interviews. When you market yourself personally by direct mail, the only items the interviewer has to decide if you will be interviewed are your resume and cover letter. If these are good, you will get interviews—if they are inadequate, you probably won't. Make a point of asking experienced people to review both documents for you. Have these individuals help you reconstruct the resume, rewrite the cover letter, and review the process you will follow when they are mailed. You may find that some cosmetic changes can produce more favorable results.

In fact, consider rewriting the cover letter and resume and sending it to companies you have already previously approached. Of course, some time should elapse between mailings, but a direct mail overture three months after the initial unsuccessful contact might, from a timing point of view, hit the target. There are a number of reasons why a company might have an opening today that didn't exist a few months before.

Your lack of success in getting a great job may not involve failing to get great job interviews but instead how you handle the interviews and the follow-up process after you get them. For some thoughts on this subject, read the chapter that follows, entitled "Postscript."

Finally, I would strongly suggest you reread this book! No matter how carefully you read a book, you can't absorb it all in one sitting. A second (or third) reading will highlight important points overlooked in the first reading.

22. Postscript

Because of your efforts and the knowledge you have gained from this book, you have succeeded in lining up a number of interviews for excellent positions. And in the very competitive world of job seeking for college graduates, that's great.

But I must tell you that your preparation work is not over. True, you have more and better interviews than your associates, but what happens after the interview is set up is also important. *GET THAT INTERVIEW!: The Indispensable Guide for College Grads* promised to bring you to this point but did not promise to take you further—through the job interview to being hired. And that is an important subject—one that could make or break your employment chances.

Before you actually have an interview, I strongly urge you to read one or more books on how to handle yourself in an interview. As one noted authority has said, once an interview is arranged, your continued success in the job quest is based mostly on how well you handle the interview and its related activities. In other words, the content of your resume, cover letter, and prospecting approach gets you the interview, but how you handle yourself in the interview process gets you the job.

Recommended Reading

Adams, Bob and Linda Morin. *The Complete Resume and Job Search Book For College Students*. Holbrook: Adams, Inc. MA, 1992.

Barkley, Nella. *How to Help Your Child Land the Right Job (Without Being a Pain in the Neck)*. New York: Workman Publishing Co., Inc., 1993.

Bouchard, Jerry. *Graduating to the 9 to 5 World*. Manassas: Impact Publications, 1991.

Briggs, James I. and Robert B. Nelson. *The Berkeley Guide to Employment for New College Graduates*. Berkeley: Ten Speed Press, 1984.

Cohen, William A. *The Student's Guide to Finding a Superior Job*. 2d ed. San Diego: Avant Books, 1993.

Dehner, Mary. *How to Move From College into a Secure Job*. Lincolnwood: VGM Career Books, 1994.

Falvey, Jack. *After College: The Business of Getting Jobs*. Charlotte: Williamson Publishing Co., 1986.

Fox, Dr. Marcia R. *Put Your Degree to Work: The New Professional's Guide to Career Planning and Job Hunting*. 2d ed. W.W. Norton & Co., Inc., 1988.

Fry, Ron. *Your 1st Interview*. 2d ed. Hawthorne: Career Press, Inc., 1993.

Osher, Dr. Bill and Sioux Henley Campbell. *The Blue Chip Graduate: A Four-Year College Plan for Career Success*. Atlanta: Peachtree Publishers, Ltd., 1987.

Phifer, Paul. *College Majors and Careers: A Resource Guide for Effective Life Planning*. Rev. ed. Garrett Park: Garrett Park Press, 1993.

Resumes for College Students and Other Recent Graduates. Lincolnwood: VGM Career Books, 1992.

Schmidt, Peggy. *Making It on Your First Job: When You're Young, Ambitious and Inexperienced*. Princeton: Peterson's Guides, Inc., 1991.

Schuman, Nancy and Adele Lewis. *From College to Career: Winning Resumes for College Graduates*. Hauppauge: Barron's Educational Series, Inc., 1993.

Shingleton, John D. *Career Planning for the 1990's: A Guide for Today's Graduates*. Garrett Park: Garrett Park Press, 1991.

Stoodley, Martha. *Information Interviewing: What Is It and How to Use It in Your Career*. Garrett Park: Garrett Park Press, 1990.

Strassor, Dr. Stephen and John Sena. *From Campus to Corporation*. Hawthorne: Career Press, Inc., 1990.

Tener, Elizabeth. *The Smith College Job Guide: How to Find and Manage Your First Job*. New York: Plume Books, 1991.

INDEX

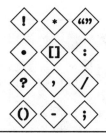

BARRON'S POCKET GUIDES—

The handy, quick-reference tools that you can count on—no matter where you are!

ISBN: 4843-1
$6.95 Canada $8.50

ISBN: 4285-9
$6.95 Canada $8.95

ISBN: 4381-2
$6.95 Canada $7.95

ISBN: 4404-5
$5.95 Canada $7.95

ISBN: 4845-8
$7.95 Canada $10.50

ISBN: 4380-4
$6.95 Canada $8.95

ISBN: 4382-0
$6.95 Canada $8.95

ISBN: 4488-6
$5.95 Canada $7.95

BARRON'S BARRON'S EDUCATIONAL SERIES, INC.
250 Wireless Boulevard • Hauppauge, New York 11788
In Canada: Georgetown Book Warehouse
34 Armstrong Avenue • Georgetown, Ontario L7G 4R9   ISBN PREFIX : 0-8120

Prices subject to change without notice. Books may be purchased at your bookstore, or by mail from Barron's. Enclose check or money order for total amount plus 10% for postage and handling (minimum charge $3.75, Can. $4.00). New York state residents add sales tax. All books are paperback editions.

(#18) R 4/95

BUSINESS ENGLISH

Second Edition • Andrea B. Geffner

DEVELOP EFFECTIVE BUSINESS WRITING SKILLS

BASIC RULES OF GRAMMAR AND USAGE
Subject and Verb • Sentence Structure • Punctuation • Abbreviation • Commonly Confused Words

MASTER EVERY CATEGORY OF BUSINESS CORRESPONDENCE
Memos • Letters • Reports • Models of each category show correct formats

NEW IN THIS EDITION
Advice for using electronic media • Guidelines for writing effective proposals

EXERCISES AND PRACTICE CORRESPONDENCE

BARRON'S

$12.95   Canada $16.95

Barron's Educational Series, Inc.
250 Wireless Boulevard, Hauppauge, NY 11788
In Canada: Georgetown Book Warehouse
34 Armstrong Avenue, Georgetown, Ont. L7G 4R9
(#31) R 9/95

TITLES THAT GENERATE SUCCESS!

Business Success Series

Fifteen titles comprise Barron's innovative series designed to help the business person succeed! Seasoned professionals offer commonsense advice and facts on how to master job techniques that will generate success. Each book: Paperback, $4.95, Can. $6.50, 96 pp., 4 $^3/_{16}$" × 7"

Conduct Better Job Interviews (4580-7)
Conquering Stress (4837-7)
Creative Problem Solving (1461-8)
Delegating Authority (4604-8)
How To Negotiate a Bigger Raise (4604-8)
Make Presentations With Confidence (4588-2)
Maximizing Your Memory Power (4799-0)
Motivating People (4792-3)
Projecting a Positive Image (1455-3)
Running a Meeting That Works (4640-4)
Speed Reading (1845-1)
Time Management (4792-3)
Using the Telephone More Effectively (4672-2)
Winning With Difficult People (4583-1)
Writing Effective Letters and Memos (4674-9)

Prices subject to change without notice. Books may be purchased at your bookstore or by mail from Barron's. Enclose check or money order for total amount plus sales tax where applicable and 10% for postage and handling (minimum charge of $3.75, Canada $4.00).
ISBN PREFIX: 0-8120

Barron's Educational Series, Inc.
250 Wireless Blvd., Hauppauge, NY 11788
In Canada: Georgetown Warehouse
34 Armstrong Ave., Georgetown, Ont. L7G 4R9

#53
R 3/95